SCIENTIFIC HYPNOTISM

SCIENTIFIC HYPNOTISM

AN INTRODUCTORY SURVEY OF THEORY AND PRACTICE

by

RALPH B. WINN, Ph.D.
DEPARTMENT OF PSYCHOLOGY
COLLEGE OF THE CITY OF NEW YORK

THORSONS PUBLISHERS LIMITED
Wellingborough, Northamptonshire

Originally published in the U.S.A.
First United Kingdom Edition February 1958
Second Impression October 1965
Third Impression December 1970
Fourth Impression April 1975

ISBN 0 7225 0063 7

Printed and bound in Great Britain by
Whitstable Litho Limited, Whitstable,
Kent

Foreword

The subject of hypnosis needed to be taken off of the vaudeville stage, out of the laboratory, and into the minds of thoughtful persons everywhere. The present well known work SCIENTIFIC HYPNOTISM has been a pioneer in this field.

Its merits are solid and various. It begins by showing that the phenomena of hypnotism are not mystical but natural. As such, they are susceptible to scientific analysis as well as control.

The author then arouses our interest by proceeding to give one of the best descriptions of hypnotic wonders in the literature of hypnosis. These, he shows, are closely connected with hysteria, and with the still better known effects of suggestion and emotion. His running account of all these effects makes the reader feel he owes it to himself to grasp the situation.

Indeed, we ourselves feel that the central part of the nervous system is just as much involved in hypnotic effects as is the autonomic part (of the peripheral nervous system). This serves to make the facts of hypnotism still more remarkable. We may well believe Dr. Winn when he says, "Hypnotism . . . puts at the disposal of science the greatest power yet known of influencing human minds . . ." (p. 43).

As interesting as the first part of the book "Theory" is, we feel that the part on "Practice" is still more absorbing. Dr. Winn, a professional hypnotist as well as a professor of psychology, has had much practical experience, and in his chapter "How To Hypnotize," he gives several advanced pointers that are usually ignored. The great importance of post-hypnotic suggestions, as yet not fully explored, is urged. (We feel that self-hypnosis, with regular "booster meetings" given by the hypnotist himself to the individual, is a rich and undeveloped field.)

Winn's chapter on "Oneirosis," a form of light hypnotism, makes us begin to realize how we can use this great force in everyday living. Indeed, its influence for good is just beginning to dawn upon men!

This influence will be exerted, says our author, in three main ways; increasingly in medicine and psychology, but . . . and here is the surprise—especially in education! This closing part of his book should give school administrators a start. We are interested in what readers think of this bold new theory, and would like to hear from them in writing, on the matter.

And so, success to your vivid adventure, in the reading journey at hand.

MELVIN POWERS

CONTENTS

INTRODUCTION

Many sciences began in superstition, perhaps because knowledge seldom arises by itself, but requires a great deal of patience and caution and also of wisdom grown out of continual disappointments. Ignorance coupled with imagination is satisfied with superstition much better than with truth at the earlier stages of human civilization. There was, for instance, a time when people feeling sick went to, or sent for, a medicine man. He would appear, dressed in a manner appropriate to his position of prestige, make a few mysterious signs, mumble some incoherent words intended to chase evil spirits away, and leave a "prescription" consisting of powdered roots, dried leaves, or some indescribable concoction. Assisted by faith, the patient would recover. Or . . . he would die.

Superstition in regard to health and disease still prevails in the less civilized countries of the world. Years ago I came across a tribe, in Eastern Africa, which claimed to know a sure remedy against rabies. When a man was bitten by a mad dog, he would kill the animal and hurry with its body to the medicine man who immediately proceeded to administer the solemn treatment prescribed by an ancient tradition. First of all, the victim was made to eat a piece of the dead dog's raw flesh. As soon as this, part of the treatment was completed, he was given a slice of bread and some bluish substance, supposedly a powdered root, which had to be consumed right on the spot, lest the great secret of cure be divulged. Finally, the fellow was dismissed satisfied. The natives asserted that fatal results were infrequent; many of them swore that death never occurred as a result. But my unprejudiced observation showed that the victim usually died within a month or so, presumably from another cause.

Even in Europe scientific acquaintance with the human body, its structure and functions, and with diseases affecting it, is of a comparatively recent date. In retrospection, medieval physicians did not differ much from pagan shamans, and prayer was still one of the best "remedies." When medicine finally made its appearance, populace, incited by adherents to the old ways, fought the new ideas bitterly and stubbornly. Anatomists seeking the secrets of bodily structure had to perform their research and to satisfy their scientific curiosity in utmost secrecy; for, if found out by the authorities or clergy, they would have to pay the penalty of humiliation, exile, or even torture and death. Vivisection was unconditionally condemned as thoroughly immoral and as a grave sin against the ancient dogmata of religion. The sanitary methods of surgery, even if known, were banned as a dangerous innovation.

The picture of modern life is quite different, but it has its own superstitions. Some old prejudices may have been totally eradicated, but new ones have taken their place. Vaccination is still being fought in semi-civilized countries as a diabolical innovation. Opposition to eugenics and birth-control is often of a similar origin even in our own land. Sex remains a thing of shame. Though in novel forms, conservatism retains a powerful hold on the community, not excluding its medical representatives.

Whatever be its social deficiencies, the science of medicine has gained a decisive victory over the chauvinism of its learned enemies and over the mental inertness of the masses. It now brings life, health and happiness to countless men, women and children. It demonstrates its miraculous proficiency by alleviating the cruel pains of childbirth, by preventing dangerous epidemics, by performing intricate operations, by extending the span of human life. Though magic has never completely relinquished its grasp on the ignorant, credulous and fraudulent, it continues to recede more and more into the fading background of obscure practices. Medicine is truly a science today.

Again, there was a time when the study of stars and planets was the province of influential magi and astrologists. They had developed an extensive pseudo-science that claimed the power of divining the future of men, of predicting the course of events, and of guiding the destiny of empires. Solemn and mighty, the astrologists prepared complicated charts, speculated on the signs of the Zodiac, wrote about a mysterious connection of stars with birth and death, and jealously preserved their occult wisdom from the fresh air of courageous and unbiassed thinking. Kings and nobles sought their advice and gave, out of respect mixed with fear, a generous financial support to their enterprise. Astrology became a lucrative occupation, with professional secrets transmitted from generation to generation.

But the day of the magi has passed. Their prestige has fallen low. Statesmen and merchants no longer seek their advice.   Newsstands and libraries, it is true, still carry a considerable supply of literature dealing with astrology.   But the masters of this ancient art have come to share their place and income with gypsy fortune-tellers and phrenologists, assembling their clientele from among the least intelligent and the most superstitious.

Out of the ashes left by the decay of astrology, there arose the body of astronomical knowledge.   Its claims may be comparatively modest, but they are simple, serious and trustworthy.   The new science rendered no lip-service to kings and nobles; it renounced mysticism; it acknowledged its total inability to predict and control changes in personal life.   At first, it shocked many a man by demonstrating that the earth is merely a tiny speck of matter lost in the enormous spaces of the universe.   But gradually people got accustomed to appreciate the power of scientific argument and calculation.   Astronomy gave us a deep understanding of, and vast information concerning, the motions of heavenly bodies, the composition of stars, and the laws of cosmic change.   It taught us to face eclipses and comets with interest rather than with fear.   Astronomy came to stay and to grow.

Alchemy is one more example of the lowly origin of great sciences.   Centuries ago, when information concerning elements and their combinations was scanty and largely faulty, mysticism pervaded this field of study. The wizards of ancient laboratories, not unlike medicine men, possessed some valuable knowledge.   But, in comparison with the modern wealth of reliable data, this knowledge was extremely limited, even though its claims were great. Driven by the wild flame of imagination and by the enduring hope of enrichment, the alchemists vainly sought "the philosopher's stone" and fruitlessly experimented in striving to effect the transmutation of common elements into gold. They worked inspired by faith, not by understanding.

Today, the science of chemistry has practically banished the obsolete methods of alchemy. In their stead, it has developed new and feasible approaches to the study of the composition and transformation of matter. Among its many attainments is the realized dream of transmuting elements, though gold cannot yet be manufactured in laboratories. Chemistry has even a superior achievement to its credit. It has become an inseparable friend of industry and agriculture; in many instances it has created new industries. It has given men, in fact, such power and mastery over natural forces as could not have occurred to the mind of a most imaginative alchemist.

Contrary to the pre-scientific arts of medicine, astrology and alchemy, the modern sciences promise no miracles. Nevertheless, their real strength and accomplishments are by far superior to those of magic. Where magic boasted, science works. True as this is, the experience of progressive thought was a continuous struggle against the recurrent tendency of human nature, especially among superficially educated people, to discover mystery in anything that, to their mind, appears unusual. The fight science waged against ignorance, superstition and mysticism is not over; as it seems, the fight must be carried on. For some of the newer sciences, like their older predecessors, began in wonder.

One of the fields where, unfortunately, much of the ancient magic tenaciously persists is that of hypnotism.

Few can resist the thrill aroused by a demonstration of hypnosis.[1]   Sensing this public attitude, the adventurers of research as well as the exploiters of human credulity are in the habit of coloring their demonstrations with a touch of the supernatural and occult. They glean notoriety, while the pursuit of truth is impeded. As a result, some scholars are themselves carried away by the contagion of excitement and become addicts to mysticism; others, repelled by the atmosphere of superstition, pass by in disgust and disapproval.

However, underneath the sensational appearance, there is nothing miraculous about the phenomena of hypnosis. It is important for scientific men to recognize this fact, before they can free themselves from mysticism in investigation as well as from the opposite (negative) prejudice that the phenomena of suggestion are not worthy of scientific attention. When a problem had been interpreted in a wrong way, the scientist is not justified to turn his mind away from it in disgust. He must face it and correct whatever mistakes had been committed.   The truth remains that everything in nature deserves serious and accurate study, and that every phenomenon is natural. Such recognition is the first principle of scientific method and the chief prerequisite for all fruitful and careful research. A talented observer converted to mysticism ceases to be a scientist. Let there be no mistake, science comes not to promote but to destroy superstition. And now let us keep in mind that *the phenomena underlying the field of hypnotism are natural.*

---

[1] I follow other authorities on the subject in distinguishing between *hypnotism,* as a body and field of knowledge, and *hypnosis,* as a phenomenon and state.

One hundred and fifty years ago F. A. Mesmer (1733–1815), a Viennese physician, attempted to raise the art of suggestion to the level of practical science. But the flavor of magic was strong with him, just as it was strong with many of his successors. A believer in a causal connection between heavenly bodies and human lives, Mesmer revived the spirit of ancient astrology and taught that there exists "a fluid universally diffused, so continuous as not to admit of a vacuum, incomparably subtle, and naturally susceptible of receiving, propagating, and communicating all motor disturbances."[2] This fluid, according to Mesmer, accounted for the phenomena of magnetism; but it acquired a particular significance in the human being who has two magnetic poles (!?). As a result, "animal magnetism" becomes a power that can be accumulated, concentrated and transferred. In the process of suggestion, this magnetic fluid, possessing curative properties, emanates from the eyes and hands of the magnetist. To enhance the activity of this truly wondrous power, patients had to be magnetized themselves. This was done by means of a "baquet", a large tank filled with water, iron filings and ground glass. Special rods were attached to the baquet, and the patients had to be in contact with them, while Mesmer, in a magnificent robe, addressed them and walked around.

Mesmer's mystic attitude toward the problem of suggestion was a great misfortune, as far as serious study of the field was concerned. Hypnotism acquired a bad reputation that persisted during many years and

[2] Quoted from A. Binet and C. Féré, *Animal Magnetism,* 5. For a full statement of Mesmer's "twenty-seven propositions" see M. Goldsmith, *Franz Anton Mesmer,* 117-121.

still is not completely dispelled. To make things worse, "the later utilization of hypnotism by charlatans made every honest man extremely wary lest even his sincere interest in it bring him into disrepute."[3]

Under the pressure of expanding knowledge, however, all prejudice collapses sooner or later. The study of hypnotic phenomena bids definitely today for acceptance into the family of recognized sciences. In the manner shown by medicine, astronomy and chemistry, in their emancipation from crudity and superstition, the science of hypnotism promises to open new vistas for research and practice. To facilitate this transition—which has yet to be accomplished—it will be necessary, I believe, to forbid the practice of hypnosis to the untrained and unqualified and to discourage idle public demonstrations, at least until suggestion acquires a solid and verified foundation of knowledge.

Scholars already begin to transcend their distrust of hypnosis and to realize the coming importance of the study of suggestion. In their natural caution, they are inclined to be conservative in estimates and expectations. Perhaps this should be so. Yet every person having relevant and up-to-date knowledge feels that the theoretical and practical discoveries awaiting us, as soon as research gains in courage and depth, are likely to transcend our best hopes. In the words of one of the few scientists[4] now devoting their time and effort to the study of suggestion, "the first and last words which

---

[3] M. H. Erickson, "Possible Detrimental Effects of Experimental Hypnosis," *Journal of Abnormal and Social Psychology,* 1932.

[4] Blankfort, Michael, "Why We Don't Know Much About Hypnosis," *Journal of Abnormal and Social Psychology,* 1932. A similar position was taken, among other psychologists, by T. Ribot, H. Muensterberg, W. McDougall, and C. Hull.

can be said of hypnosis is that it is the most interesting and most profound of all psychological material which has merited so little attention."

Are the above claims justified? Does hypnotism, indeed, offer data of genuine scientific importance and a method of great practical value?

PART I

THEORY

CHAPTER I

A Few Facts About Hypnosis

Whenever I am approached with questions concerning hypnotism, I observe a good deal of curiosity as well as of skepticism. People are eager to see how I do it. They expect to witness something spectacular, extraordinary; to be thrilled and entertained; or else to have new food for ridicule, for wisecracks. But I do not handle that sort of goods. I merely try to comprehend phenomena underlying the field and to explain their significance. Consequently, I seldom meet persons who are not, at first, disappointed with my attitude of scientific caution and with the strict process of logical speculation. They came to watch an amusing demonstration, something to talk about, but received a lecture. Nevertheless, once the sharp feeling of disappointment is over, some of the original interest is regained, but now it is scientific rather than idle. For facts concerning hypnosis and suggestion are so significant and yet so simple that, properly grouped and presented, they cannot help but arouse intelligent people to wondering and thinking.

A few examples will help illustrate the nature of hypnotic phenomena. Time: early fall. Place: New York City. A subject is hypnotized in an ordinary room, with normal temperature, and the following suggestion is given to him in a calm yet emphatic voice:

"Let me take a look at the weather report for today. Ah, fair and warmer. It certainly is warmer, much warmer. Do you mind if I take off my coat? I do not recall, you know, a hotter day in the City. Not for several years, at least. It is surely above 90, perhaps above 100. In a tropical country, say in the West Indies, I should not be surprised. There you expect it, you get used to it. And, of course, you wear clothes appropriate to the climate. But here, in New York City, it is amazingly warm for the month of September. In spite of the fact that I am lightly dressed, perspiration just flows down my face and back. Where is my handkerchief?"

The hypnotist stops for a few seconds to observe the subject and then resumes: "You look quite warm, too. You don't seem to be able to endure high temperature. No, you don't. I see beads of perspiration on your forehead. Can I do anything for you? Some lemonade? Of course. I shall be back in a minute."

He leaves the room and returns promptly with a glass of lemonade—or it might be plain water—saying: "Lemonade is very refreshing. Here it is. Take the glass. I am sure you'll like it."

As the experimenter proceeds with the monologue, the subject clearly develops the appearance of a man suffering from intense heat. He gets uneasy and, true enough, perspiration bedews his face. Nothing surprising, one may remark: he has merely received a suggestion and has reacted to it in a natural way. This is precisely my contention: the phenomenon is a natural reaction to suggestion under hypnosis. But this reaction, though quite normal under the circumstances, is not one you can reproduce by an effort of conscious will. Try, indeed, with all the imagination you possess, to develop sweat by a sheer strain of your fancy. It simply cannot be done. Obviously, we have witnessed a case of auto-suggestion considerably intensified by means of hypnosis. It brought into operation certain natural powers of the subject's body, making the imaginary experience sufficiently realistic to evoke drops of sweat out of the pores of his skin.

Take another case. The newspapers reported some time ago that three investigators from Wayne University (Drs. Frick, Patterson and Scantlebury) had performed a highly interesting experiment. First they made a subject fast for twenty hours, which is a sufficiently long period to arouse any healthy person's appetite. At the end of the period, the subject was hypnotized and a purely imaginary meal was offered to him. The suggestion, obviously, produced a complete illusion, for the man went through all the customary movements of mastication and swallowing. Throughout the experiment, I assume, he was given guiding suggestions, in the form of verbal description of the courses. To make the case even more interesting, the subject appeared to be quite satisfied at the end of the meal. His reactions, furthermore, were not confined to reproducing the outward act of eating. There was no sign of pretense.   The experimenters demonstrated, in fact, that the effects of their suggestion went far beyond ordinarily observed motions.   The behavior of the subject's stomach was, too, typical of a person satisfying his hunger.   Its contractions went through the regular cycle of peristaltic movements which normally accompany the consumption of a substantial dinner.   And from what we have learned from Pavlov's studies of the conditioned reflex, we are fully justified in assuming that the salivary glands and pancreas of the subject poured their juices into the mouth and gastrointestinal tract, according to all the laws of human physiology.   The illusion was complete, in mind and body.

The experiment was not altogether new, for similar observations had been reported before, under various conditions, by Luckhardt and Johnston,[1] Heilig and Hoff,[2] Delougne and Hansen.[3]   Appetite was known to be re-aroused by a suggestion given immediately after a meal, or stopped just before it.   The movements of the bowels were similarly regulated, within limits, by Krafft-Ebing, Forel, Moll, and others.   A sea-voyage could be drawn before the mind of a hypnotized subject, with such realism as to make him feel nauseated and show all the symptoms of sea-sickness.

A few other examples of what can be done by means of hypnotic suggestion can be cited in brief.

---

[1] "The Psychic Secretion of Gastric Juice under Hypnosis," *American Journal of Physiology,* 1924.

[2] "Beitraege zur hypnotischen Beeinflussung der Magenfunktion," *Medizinische Klinik,* 1925.

[3] "Die suggestive Beeinflussbarkeit der Magen und Pankreassekretion in der Hypnose," *Deutsches Archiv f. Klinische Medizin,* 1927.

People can be made *to see* things which are not present or *not to see* objects in front of them. The experience produced in this manner may not be identical in kind with that of the ordinary waking state, but its realism is surely comparable to the realism of dreams. Thus, the sun will shine at night for the subject, and stars will be visible while the eyes are closed. The hallucinations resulting from hypnotic suggestion are even more convincing when the subject moves about. Then he behaves as if he actually saw things which are not there or as if he did not see objects before him, depending on the suggestion. In one experiment, for instance, a man was made "to walk into the wall from which he sustained a nose bleed when told to walk through an imaginary door in the wall."[4]

Hallucinations of sound can be produced, and the subject will listen to a symphony in a complete silence around him. When aroused from the state, he may report on the particular piece of music he was listening to; naturally, this will happen only if the subject is familiar with the piece suggested during the trance. Or, the opposite sort of illusion can be created, so that he will utterly disregard a loud voice calling him by his first name. The same effect can be occasionally produced also in the post-hypnotic state. At a recent meeting of the American Psychiatric Association, M. H. Erickson reported that complete physical deafness had been produced and removed in two college students solely by hypnotic suggestion.

Persons have been known to drink kerosene or diluted ink with apparent pleasure, as if it were wine, tea or

---

[4] R. M. Dorcus and G. W. Shaffer, *Textbook of Abnormal Psychology*, 1934, p. 192.

milk, depending on the suggestion. Persons have been known to turn away with the expression of disgust on their faces from an excellent perfume; or to inhale with delight the vapors from a bottle of ammonia. Perception, evidently, is subject to serious modification in hypnosis.

Krafft-Ebing made his subjects develop goose-pimples by suggesting a cold bath to them; also to lower or raise their bodily temperature, in accordance with his directions. Bramwell changed the rate of pulsation, to range on different occasions between sixty and over one hundred beats per minute. Eichelberg caused fever, in the same manner. Skin blisters were produced by suggesting a burn in experiments undertaken independently by Wetterstrand, Schrenck-Notzing, Delboeuf, C. Kreibich, F. Heller, and others. Even time could be regulated in some instances almost to the minute when blisters were to appear.

Braid is known to have performed the following remarkable experiment:[5] "He hypnotized a patient who was nursing, and suggested an increased secretion of milk in one breast. On awaking she had no recollection of what had been done, but complained of a feeling of tightness and tension in the breast. Her husband then told her that Braid had been trying to increase the secretion of milk. She was sceptical as to the result, as the child was fourteen months old and the milk had almost disappeared. Her breast, however, almost immediately became distended with milk, and a few days later she complained that her figure was deformed in consequence. Braid again hypnotized her and suc-

---

[5] As reported by Bramwell, *Hypnotism*, 88.

cessfully repeated the experiment with the other breast. The patient suckled her child for six months longer, the supply of milk being more abundant than it had been at any time since her confinement." The opposite kind of experiment, to stop the accumulation of milk, was performed by many hypnotists, among them by Esdaile, Mohr and Heyer. In most instances, the mother had suffered pains in the breasts, having lost the baby.

All the above observations, and many others of similar character, have been made by reliable authorities and repeatedly verified. Several of them have been once or more reproduced in my own experiments. Striking they may be, yet there is nothing miraculous about them. There is no need to invoke a supernatural agency for their explanation. The mystery of nature is invariably the ignorance of men, be it justifiable or not. Nothing miraculous or unnatural, indeed, can be attained by hypnotic procedure. It deals with, and is limited by, certain powers within the human organism, that can be made to work once we know how to stimulate the mechanism involved in its activities. However, as the effects described above cannot be produced at will, merely by wishing for their appearance, it is obvious that hypnosis implies some physiological mechanism which is not open to a direct voluntary control. This mechanism will determine what can and what can not be accomplished by means of hypnosis.

Much and varied evidence is available in support of the belief that the bodily mechanism underlying hypnosis is identical with that involved in ordinary waking suggestion. It is hardly necessary to embark upon a detailed theoretical discussion of the problem, or even to study countless medical records. It will be sufficient to consider the following simple facts, to recognize this identity.

A number of years ago, I entered a grocery store to buy a few tomatoes, my favorite vegetable. As I was selecting them, I happened to turn over one large tomato, right in time to see a large, fat worm crawl out of it. It was silly, of course, to allow myself to be influenced by this sight—I did not buy *that* tomato, after all—but the fact remains that I could not eat any tomatoes that day and for the subsequent year. The mere sight of tomatoes would invariably bring back the recollection . . . and disgust. Even today I have not completely regained my former predilection for the vegetable. As a psychologist, I should have known how to combat the unpleasant association created by my experience in the grocery store. But psychologists, I presume, are as helpless in fighting some mental weaknesses as physicians are in overcoming some bodily ailments.   Anyway,   the   auto-suggestive   influences generated by the memorable tomato were powerful enough to modify my taste for a long time, if not for ever.

A somewhat more striking case was reported to me by a student of mine, which I shall relate in his own words: "One of my friends desired to learn to read the medical thermometer. I inserted an oral thermometer into his mouth in order that his temperature might be recorded. It remained there for about a minute when I told him that he was using a rectal thermometer. He became very much excited. In a few seconds he began to vomit profusely." I do not recall the purpose of this experiment; perhaps, there was none. But even if it was merely a practical joke, the student surely should be forgiven, for the sake of science.

Such everyday instances are familiar to most of us and could be multiplied without end. The trained nurses know that a patient, after several weeks of periodical morphine injections, will feel genuine relief from his pains when simple water is injected hypodermically, provided he does not suspect the substitution of the drug. Rashes have been known to break out, only as a result of apprehension that one had contracted some contagious disease or had handled poison ivy. People commonly develop sea-sickness *before* the boat has actually left the harbor. Fear of the dark is likely to accelerate the heart beat, even though the terrors of night are purely imaginary.

H. F. Dunbar cites[6] an interesting case of "grossesse nerveuse", which shows how deeply can imagination modify the bodily functions; she writes: "E. Graefenberg (1929) was called to a delivery one morning at five o'clock, only to find a midwife who had been waiting forty eight hours and a physician who had been waiting twenty four hours for the final termination of labor. The patient, forty five years old, was lying in bed shaken by almost continuous bearing-down pains. . . This woman who had wished all her life for a child had succumbed to an idea of pregnancy." Autosuggestion could make the body simulate the symptoms of pregnancy and deceive two specialists; but it could not produce the baby.

A remarkable case is related by Woodson. A patient suffered from dementia praecox (paranoid type), imag-

---

[6] *Emotions and Bodily Changes*, 346-47.

ining that the upper part of his body was as solid within
as concrete.   The author contends that the patient died
in consequence of this delusion.   He says:[7]

"And the Concrete Man is gone also.   The Gray
Wagon made another trip.   Death ended his delusion
that he was doomed to live for a thousand years.   I
wonder if he is glad at the release.   He had sought
death by physical means; he achieved it through a state
of mind.   His hallucination that he was solid concrete
from the neck down prevented his body from assimilat-
ing the food which the attendants forcibly fed him.   His
mind finally starved him to death.

"Yes indeed; the mind which motivates and regulates
bodily functions can as readily wreck them.   Those of
us who live among the insane see that demonstrated
almost daily; demonstrated beyond cavil of question.
Wreck that part of your brain which motivates the
heartbeat and the heartbeat stops, whether the weapon
is a bullet or an hallucination.

"While those on the outside are arguing as to
whether the mind can cause or cure organic troubles, we
on the inside are unalterably convinced that it can.
We do not know whether a conscious effort of the will
can do so, but most of us believe that it can, at least to
some extent."

Mr. Woodson's contention is clearly unscientific and
should be taken with a grain of salt.   I am unwilling to
accept all the implications of his description.   It surely
is unnecessary to believe that the Concrete Man died
solely as a result of his peculiar delusion.   Nor can we
deny a certain naiveté of Mr. Woodson's assumptions.

---

[7] *Behind the Door of Delusion,* 144.

Nevertheless, his story provides us with a startling illustration as to dependence of health upon one's mental state. Thoughts as well as emotions do influence bodily metabolism. The state of mind can, indeed, "cause or cure organic troubles." Who has not seen, in fact, persons who virtually "blossom out" after having won success or happiness? And who has not seen them, as it were, wither away under the pressure of failure? Who does not recall the bodily radiance of a couple in love? And who can forget the sight of a mother actually perishing from grief after the loss of her only child? Every physician or nurse knows that, in combating a serious disease, consideration and tact are essential. Life hanging on a thin thread may turn one way or another, depending upon the patient's mental attitude. And this is open to suggestion. It may be criminal to tell him the plain but cruel truth. A white lie, consolation, and encouragement should be given him, not to soothe his suffering, but to give strength and support to his mind and also to his body. Medicine has at its disposal the weapons of laboratory, surgery, pharmacology, and psychology. None of these should be neglected.

There is a power of mind over body that cannot be denied. It used to be conceived as a mystical influence of the disembodied soul upon mortal flesh. Science offers us a more reliable explanation. We have already repeatedly intimated that there exists a bodily mechanism responsible for this connection. We observed that, under the pressure of a powerful and appropriate suggestion, almost any part of the organism may begin to act in a fashion which under no circumstance can be reproduced at will. It does not matter whether the change takes place under hypnosis or in an ordinary waking state. In either case suggestion is operative. In fact, many of the phenomena commonly observed under hypnosis have also been seen apart from it, in the normal state of high suggestibility, or in the abnormal state of hysteria. The question that stands before us is then: *What is the bodily mechanism underlying these phenomena?*

CHAPTER II

THE BODILY MECHANISM OF SUGGESTION

When we consider the enormous multiplicity of bodily processes that take place in the human organism at all times, day or night, it becomes obvious that conscious attention can be given only to a small part of them. As far as the great mass of bodily activities are concerned, they are performed despite or independently of human volition. As in the case of digestion, they do not require the cooperation of human consciousness; they can be performed without its assistance. In some instances, in fact, conscious attention actually disturbs the coordination of physiological processes. And surely, there is nothing abnormal or harmful in the fact that, in addition to its voluntary activities, our organism is capable of handling most of its complex tasks in an automatic, mechanical fashion. Quite the contrary, this is truly wonderful, because how else could these numerous tasks be adequately performed?

Suppose the organism had to take care of every motion and functional act by a special effort of will. How hopeless the task would be! A simple process of walking would resolve into an unbelievably tedious and awkward complexity of muscular contractions, relaxations, and coordinations. Assuming it to be possible at all, it would take a much longer time to learn how to operate them consciously and deliberately than the time a child requires to learn how to walk. And what

about the processes within the body, so essential to life?
We should not even know what to do with our intestines
and glands to digest a little food! How much saliva is
needed to make a meal digestible? How much bile?
What is the best way of distributing the blood supply?
We might even forget to make the heart beat while we
sleep! There are, in addition, countless other organs,
tissues, processes needing constant control and regulation. Our body knows obviously better than our mind
the practical anatomy and physiology of the organism,
especially in its minute details. The fact is that the
muscles, nerves, blood vessels, and various organs are
well adjusted and qualified for the performance of their
natural and specific functions. We could not improve
upon their control and regulation.

Thus it happens that we are able to relax, let the
mind stray and wander, and yet everything will be taken
care of. The stomach will continue, unassisted, to perform its gastric duties. The heart will mark its even
beat. Veins will go on carrying blood. And the re-
mainder of the system, with parts and organs so minute
as to be invisible to the naked eye and so numerous as
to be beyond enumeration, will carry on in a manner
so remarkable that the wheels of the largest factory in
the world are a mere child's toy in comparison.

How shall we explain this miraculous organization
and this smooth performance of the human body, that
in normal conditions helps maintain life and daily
struggle for three or four score years? Where shall we
locate the central automatic control, the neural "switch-
board" that accounts for the feat? An important role
is played in these activities, doubtless, by innate properties of the cells and tissues themselves. But the co-

ordination of organic functions is achieved mainly by the brain and the network of fibres connecting it with every organ and every part of the body. Over 12,000,-000,000 cells—six times the number of human beings in the entire world—are thus engaged in the administration of a single organism, both conscious and mechanical. Conscious activities may be responsible for the growth of our civilization, but mechanical activities are by far the more important in the question of the continuity of biological life.

In the course of ages, the human organism has worked out two distinct ways of handling its intricate tasks. When concerned with a novel situation, which has to be discerned, evaluated, understood, in short, when a conscious adjustment is to be made, the phenomenon is isolated and focused by attention for special consideration. It may consist in watching, listening, recalling, planning, reasoning. When, on the other hand, a particular type of activity becomes both indispensable and habitual, it is transformed into a part of the bodily mechanism and is henceforth performed involuntarily, along with habits formed before. As far as most biologically important processes are concerned, they are automatic from birth.

The distinction is exemplified in countless ways. Some actions are subject to voluntary control. I decide to mail a letter, for instance, and proceed to leave the house. Or I do not feel like walking and stay at home. I am interested in a discussion, join it and carry it on. Or I remain silent. I do as I please. Other actions, on the other hand, are subject to involuntary control. I am afraid that I might blush, for example, but my ears get red nevertheless. I wish I could develop an appetite, but it fails to come. I should like to gain additional weight, but my mind has no direct control over my digestion and metabolism.

Nature has found it necessary to relegate most visceral activities to unconscious regulation, so as to enable consciousness to take better care of important new adjustments. Nature did not plan or deliberate, of course; its marvelous biological achievements are simply a result of selective forces that defeat and destroy everything that is "irrational," in the sense of being unadjusted to existing conditions. Anyway, man finds himself in possession of a body that works largely automatically. In everyday life, this mechanization of bodily activities is attained not only by means of innate neural connections and cellular reactions; they are constantly assisted also by habituation, which is a way of liberating attention from the burden of countless pressing tasks.

Thus, the maximum of efficiency and economy of effort are combined through the coexistence of the conscious and unconscious neural mechanisms within one and the same organism. They constitute two interconnected and interdependent nervous systems, central and autonomic.

The *central* (also called cerebro-spinal or sensori-motor) *nervous system* is inseparably bound up with conscious and voluntary activities. The bulk of stimuli it receives comes from the sense organs, such as the eyes, ears, nose. Consequently, it carries to us the awareness of the external world, in the form of sensations of vision, hearing, smell, touch, etc. Corresponding experiences blended with memories and ideas arise in the brain. The brain, however, is not merely a receiving station; it also sends out impulses outward, towards the muscles, where decisions are transformed into actions, as when we move about our daily work, walking, talking, writing, shaking hands. Occasionally, the central nervous system is engaged in a process which we experience as thinking and which deals with the solution of countless problems of life, home, society, and science. It plays an important role also in emotions and recollections. Its activities are, as we see, quite complex and involve, directly or indirectly, the entire organism. Our purposes do not require a detailed description of the structure and functions of the brain; it will suffice to state that the central nervous system is concerned mainly with conscious experience and, particularly, with human adjustments to a changing environment.

On the other hand, breathing, digestion of food, circulation of blood and lymph, secretory functions of the glands, and in general activities concerned with the maintenance of life, are performed unconsciously, assisted by a fine mechanism of nerves, distinct from motor, sensory, and associative fibres of the central system. These nerves constitute elements of the *autonomic nervous system* (also called visceral, vegetative, or involuntary), with its two principal divisions, *sympathetic* and *parasympathetic*. It is a network of fibres, as vast, as active, and as significant (to say the least) as the other network concerned specifically with sensibility and voluntary action. Yet for some reason, whereas the central nervous system is closely studied and minutely experimented with by numerous physiologists and psychologists, "the ubiquity, the density, and the physiological importance of this dispersed

autonomous nervous system are generally underesti-
mated, even by neurologists."[1]   I daresay it is almost
completely disregarded except by a few specialists, as if
it had but a minor function to perform.   Thus R. J. A.
Berry, following Langdon Brown, sees in the autonomic nervous system merely a device designed by nature for the defense of the organism.   "The whole
nerve mechanism concerned in visceral innervation,"
says he,[2] "is protective to the organism and is an example of Nature's attempt to effect a cure by rest of the
affected part."   Now, as it stands, the statement is
decidedly ridiculous.   It would seem that the system
is useful *only* in emergency situations.   The truth is
that its primary importance lies in regulating very
ordinary and everyday processes, such as that of digestion and breathing.   Or shall we call digestion and
breathing emergency functions?   The importance of the
autonomic nervous system in emergency situations is invariably secondary, except in disease.   It is true, no
doubt, that there exists throughout the body various
adjustment organs, acting mechanically and unconsciously, of which the adrenal gland is perhaps the best
known.   Nevertheless, the system which is truly invalu-
able in emergency situations, that is to say, in novel and
trying conditions such as presented by dangers and
problems of life, is not the autonomic nervous system
at all, but, on the contrary, that great instrument of
adjustment in the animal world, the central nervous
system.   And it is this mechanism of conscious reaction
that determines what action is to be taken in emergency;

---

[1] C. J. Herrick, *An Introduction to Neurology* (5th ed.), 278.
[2] *Brain and Mind*, 99.

the normal automatic and involuntary mechanisms of adjustment become involved only subsequently.

The activities of the involuntary system are essentially reflex, but not fully independent of the higher centers of conscious reaction. In fact, the two nervous systems are closely related and are distinguished functionally rather than anatomically. Each has, however, its separate nerve fibres and centers. The fibres of the autonomic nervous system have not, to be sure, been traced as high as the cortex cerebri, although it has been shown in recent years, as Dr. L. Stone points out,[3] "that there is probably autonomic representation in the cerebral cortex itself." The anatomist can hardly be blamed for this lack of information, as it is an extraordinarily difficult work to trace microscopic fibres in the maze of nervous tissues. Consequently, more is known of the outer connections of the involuntary system, particularly, of the sympathetic trunks visible to the naked eye.

The more important visceral organs are innervated by both sympathetic and parasympathetic fibres, which generally act in the opposite way, one inhibiting and the other stimulating bodily functions. As can be easily seen from the diagram (p. 38), organs like the heart, kidneys or eyes are open to a complete involuntary regulation, practically instantaneous, by the autonomic system. The two systems, autonomic and central, are known, furthermore, to be linked at the base of the

---

[3] *The Journal of American Medical Association,* for August 1, 1936. More recently J. G. Dusser de Barenne reported to the American Association for the Advancement of Science of the existence of a "special communication sytem" between the two nervous systems, thus proving that "cortex and thalamus are in close mutual functional relation with each other."

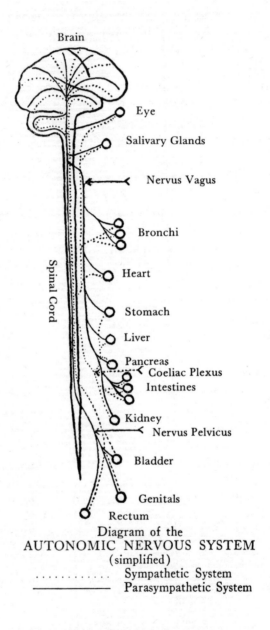

Brain

Eye

Salivary Glands

Nervus Vagus

Bronchi

Heart

Spinal Cord

Stomach

Liver

Pancreas
Coeliac Plexus
Intestines

Kidney

Nervus Pelvicus

Bladder

Genitals

Rectum

Diagram of the
AUTONOMIC NERVOUS SYSTEM
(simplified)
. . . . Sympathetic System
——————— Parasympathetic System

brain and, no doubt, in many other places less familiar to the anatomist.   The resulting interaction of voluntary and involuntary activities is ordinarily concealed, however, from consciousness, and no amount of deliberate effort is usually capable of accelerating, say, the heart-beat or of contracting blood-vessels.   The activities of most bodily organs thus remain largely mechanical and subject to influences lying beyond the ken of human will.

Yet there exist at least two channels of conscious experience by which activities of most organs, ordinarily involuntary, can be considerably influenced.   They are the channel of *emotion* and that of *suggestion* (involving imagination in various forms and degrees). Whereas no amount of conscious effort suffices to retard the periodic contractions of the intestines or to dilate blood vessels in our cheeks, fear may inhibit the peristaltics and shame will make us blush.   In many instances, it seems, involuntary reactions to emotion and suggestion are by far more dominant than voluntary ones.

The reason why so many mental diseases, particularly neuroses, originate in emotional experiences and manifest themselves in various complexes, morbid fears (phobias) and anxieties is clear: most strong feelings are experienced "all over" and find an immediate and sometimes lasting reflection in activities of practically all vital organs.   Affective states exert an especially powerful influence upon the gastro-intestinal tract. Stiller was the first, if I am not mistaken, to point out (1884)[3a] the prevalence of psychogenic dispepsias.   In

---

[3a] As reported by H. F. Dunbar in her *Emotions and Bodily Changes*, 269.

citing examples, he said: "That people develop gastric disturbances after financial losses and suffer from them until their financial conditions turn to the better, is an everyday experience." He maintained that 60 to 70 percent of all patients who consulted him for stomach ailments suffered on nervous grounds. Present figures are considerably lower, but even so physicians report[4] that one-third of digestive ailments is due to emotional difficulties, shocks and frustrations. Nor should we be surprised. "Nearly every emotional state affects the vasomotor mechanism, but each in a different manner."[5] We are able today to be even more specific and say, in general, that "pleasurable emotions promote and painful or disagreeable emotions depress the visceral functions."[6] The studies of Professor W. Cannon of Harvard University[7] have demonstrated a close connection between strong emotions and the secretion of the adrenal glands, which are innervated by the autonomic nervous system. Though no final and conclusive data are as yet available to make any positive assertions, nevertheless there are strong and numerous reasons to believe that other glands, such as the thyroid, the pituitary body, and the gonads, are also involved in our emotional life, directly or indirectly.

Emotion and suggestion are closely related. One

---

[4] J. S. McLester, "Psychic and Emotional Factors in Relation to Disorders of the Digestive Tract," *The Journal of American Medical Association,* 1927.

[5] A. Kunitz, *The Autonomic Nervous System,* 1934. p. 75. Cf.: "Perhaps every visceral function is subject to influences exerted by psychic and emotional states through the autonomic nervous system" (*ibid.,* 505).

[6] *Ibid.,* 500.

[7] Read, particularly, his *Bodily Changes in Pain, Hunger, Fear and Rage,* 1929.

commonly begets the other. Many emotional experiences, as is well known, have no clear source in the
external conditions: they seem to be fully or partly
imaginary. The fear of the dark, for instance, has no
sufficient foundation, as a rule, for its existence in
civilized conditions of life, as it had in the prehistoric
days, when the darkness of the night concealed wild
beasts and other dangerous enemies of man. Contempt
and love are often inspired by persons and objects that
are no more despicable or adorable, as the case may
be, than other similar individuals and things. The
emotion of love, particularly, is so permeated with
products of imagination that it consists largely in
creating illusions about the object of affection. Propaganda is known to arouse people to frenzy and worship, yet it attains its ends not so much through the
study or selection of facts as through utilizing the
technique of suggestion and auto-suggestion. And the
study of crowd and mob behavior shows beyond the
cavil of doubt that emotion spreads by suggestion, as it
were contagiously. This suggestive or infectious
character of emotion can be exemplified by the panic
arising in a theatre on fire, by the vicious mood of a
lynching mob, or by the mass worship of a popular
hero. Unless it be through the effect of suggestive
transmission, how can we explain, for example, the following occurrence I have come across in the newpapers?
An American traveler on his way to the Orient, if I
remember the facts correctly, got off his boat during
her stop at Genoa. It happened on the day when the
victorious troops of the Italian army returned from
Ethiopia. An enthusiastic crowd greeted the soldiers,
and the American tourist, a liberal by conviction and

no friend of Fascism, stopped to look on, as most people would. After a while, however, he suddenly realized, much to his amazement and dismay, that he had joined the crowd in shouting "Viva Mussolini!" and the like. Emotional attitudes may be, as it seems, so suggestive and contagious as to be capable of drawing a person in, with no clear realization on his part as to what is happening. Incidents of the type just described may be rare and exceptional, but the suggestiveness of emotion is an everyday experience, with its effects, visible and invisible, reaching deep into human life.

Suggestion, in its bearing upon unconscious activities of the organism, is not confined to emotions. It is a power of many forms and of considerable depth. Posthypnotic phenomena demonstrate that suggestion has a multiform and profound connection with other conscious and unconscious processes in the body. Thus, it is possible to bring forgotten experiences back to memory or to make the subject forget, for the moment, the names of his best friends. Headaches can be relieved by order of a hypnotist. The subject may be instructed to wake up the next morning at some definitely specified time, which instruction will be, in all probability, obediently executed.

The difference between the two channels by means of which the central and autonomic systems are bridged is not confined to their respective scopes. Another distinction is even more significant. Emotion, namely, in so far as it depends on the external environment for stimulation, cannot be readily controlled (except by suggestion), whereas suggestion, with the entire realm of imagination at its easy command, permits ample variation and regulation. This is the reason why hypnosis, being from the psychological standpoint merely a state of high suggestibility, offers such a fruitful field for directing and modifying human desires, attitudes and activities. Hypnotism, indeed, puts at the disposal of science the greatest power yet known of influencing human minds and the best, even if limited, way of controlling physiological functions. The extent of this power cannot be as yet estimated or measured with precision, but even the little knowledge of it we already possess makes one feel certain that potential uses and applications of hypnotic power are immense, particularly, in medicine, psychology and education.

The mechanism of suggestion is not created by hypnosis: it existed since the beginning of the human race. But the operation of the mechanism is naturally confined, in everyday experience, to special conditions of suggestive character, such as a strong emotion or faith. Hypnosis does no more than canalize this ancient channel. It creates a situation in which ordinary suggestion is magnified and opened to scientific experimentation and control.

Acting through the autonomic nervous system, suggestion can either enhance or depress normal functions of the organism. In the former case it is customary in scientific circles to speak of *excitation* (stimulation, facilitation); in the latter, of *inhibition*.

Excitation through suggestion and auto-suggestion can be best exemplified by the phenomena of appetite and sex (and other reactions based on "unconditioned reflexes," in Pavlov's terminology). Have you ever experienced a sudden flow of saliva, as you looked at somebody consuming his lunch with manifest relish right before you? If you have, then you know that various bodily activities, visible as well as invisible, which are connected with normal appetite, can be precipitated by suggestion. Have you ever seen young boys straighten their backs and look brighter, as a pretty girl comes into their presence? Or, if you still are young and healthy, have you observed introspectively that, in such cases, a feeling of increased vitality passes through you, to accelerate your thoughts and to enlighten your wits?

Inhibition through suggestion is even more interesting, from the scientific point of view, than excitation through suggestion. Though the mechanism of the phenomenon is not yet completely understood, it has been interpreted in at least four different ways, every one of which may be true, in full or in part. The depression of bodily functions can be, first of all, achieved by the counter-action of two impulses, at points of neural junction, whereby one impulse interferes with and as it were cancels another (Sherrington[8]). According to McDougall's "drainage theory," inhibition means "a switching off of the current of energy," in the way light is switched off in an electric bulb. E. D. Adrian and his followers see the cause of interference in "overcrowding." They contend that "if nerve impulses crowd on one another's heels in too rapid succession, all are extinguished."[9] Finally, inhibition may be attained by the action of chemical substances liberated within the organism. Recent studies of Drs. Cannon and Rosenblueth[10] seem to indicate the existence of

---

[8] *The Brain and Its Mechanism*, 1934. p. 12. See also his larger but older work, *The Integrative Action of the Nervous System*, 1906.
[9] E. B. Holt, *Animal Drive and the Learning Process*, 50.
[10] In the *American Journal of Physiology* and in *Endocrinology*, discussed in several issues beginning with 1932.

a substance named "sympathin" which plays an important role in the transmission and mediation of nerve impulses arising in, or dependent upon, the autonomic system. Whether or not it contains acetyl choline, a substance stimulating the parasympathetic fibres, remains to be seen.

Though the mechanism of neural excitation and inhibition is as yet imperfectly known, nevertheless its observed effects are highly significant. Some of them take most striking forms, as when perspiration, appetite, or sexual desire is aroused solely by suggestion, with no adequate cause given in sensory experience; or as when activities of the intestines are inhibited merely by the recollection of a "nauseating" experience. I do not want, however, to convey the impression that excitation and inhibition, as produced by the autonomic nervous system, are unusual phenomena. Nor that their effects are confined to involuntary activities. Quite the contrary, they modify not only mechanical processes but also conscious experience. Only striking cases of excitation and inhibition attract our attention. Ordinary cases, on the other hand, occur every day, in fact every minute, yet pass unobserved, unnoticed, as a matter of course.

Take, for instance, habits. Some of them, doubtless, are acquired or lost in a slow, gradual fashion. But then again we find habits formed, modified, or broken almost instantaneously. This may happen under the influence of a powerful suggestion or emotion, such as fear; or a more mechanical process may be responsible for the change. Professor Pavlov, starting with his doctrine that "extinction of conditioned reflexes is accompanied by inhibition," has actually developed a specific technique as to how to break habits. The truth is, in brief, that anything that has been learned, can also be unlearned either through the gradual process of obliviscence or through the abrupt process of inhibition. We forget either slowly or suddenly.

These conclusions apply also to the general problem of the inhibition (and stimulation) of memory. It is a well known fact that normal memory is able to bring back to consciousness only a small portion of what is naturally retained by the mind. This natural weakness of memory is, in a sense, an advantage, as otherwise, in an ordinary mind disinclined to, and often incapable of, giving its ideas and experiences a highly organized and systematic form, the very abundance of retained material would result in chaos, glut and confusion rather than in order and mental efficiency. The processes of evolution have led to limitations of memory and produced therefor a suitable physiological mechanism of inhibition. In exceptional instances, however, as in delirium or emotional excitement, normal memory can be stimulated to an extent almost unbelievable: this phenomenon is called *hypermnesia*. Or it can be inhibited to create a serious deficiency in the power of recall. The latter phenomenon, known as *amnesia*, may amount to an almost complete blankness in regard to the past, such as occasionally afflicts old people suffering from senility. Both types of phenomena are, in most cases, manifestations of what can be nothing else than a somewhat unusual activity of the autonomic nervous system which, evidently, has the power of inhibiting small or large portions of the field of memory or, by removing the inhibition, of restoring hidden memories to consciousness.

It is significant that, in many instances of amnesia, when the patient is, as it seems, completely unable to recall his experiences since, or prior to, the onset of the symptom, hypnosis often helps to revive his memory. The dependence of recall on suggestion, and through it on the autonomic nervous system, is thereby confirmed. In order to appreciate fully the importance of these phenomena, however, we must get acquainted with the disease called hysteria. The symptoms of this malady resemble in many respects the subject's behavior in a hypnotic trance. The parallelism is so remarkably close that it is reasonable to suspect that the bodily mechanism underlying hysteria and hypnosis is essentially the same.

CHAPTER III

HYSTERIA AND HYPNOSIS

Every once in a while we read a newspaper account of somebody who, subsequently to an emotional shock or a physical trauma, suddenly lost all the memory as to who he was and where he lived. After having stayed away from his home for weeks or even months— usually at a distance of many miles—he might recover his memory or be accidentally recognized. On having reestablished their contact with the past, such people are often able to tell their story, full or fragmentary. Take the following typical case:[1] "After a 135-mile drive of which she said she remembered nothing a woman identified as Mrs. M. of XYZ, was returned to her relatives today. 'I'm lost', she told Chief of Police W. as she stopped at police headquarters. 'I don't know where I am. The streets aren't at all familiar'. The woman, Chief W. said, was unable to identify herself and said her 'head hurts'. Dr. S. said she was suffering from amnesia. Search of a handbag revealed an automobile driver's license issued to Mrs. M. and a letter from her father. Chief W. called the father by telephone and he came for his daughter. Mrs. M. said she recalled nothing of the trip from XYZ and knew nothing of what route she took."

During the Great War, these cases of amnesia were quite common. An excellent example was reported by

---

[1] As reported in the *New York Times* for June 23, 1936.

McDougall:[2] "A color-sergeant of long service was carrying a despatch from one part of the front to another, riding a motor-bicycle. He suddenly found himself, a few hours later, pushing his bicycle through the streets of a seaport town some hundred miles from the front. He was utterly bewildered and, in order to avoid suspicion of desertion, he surrendered himself to the military police. He remained unable to give any account of his long journey from a spot near the front to the seaport. After some stay in various hospitals he came under my care. He had no symptoms beyond his amnesia for this short period of some hours' duration, and a certain depression and lack of self-confidence, such as naturally resulted from the circumstances in a man of his good record and responsible position. Waking conversation having failed to overcome the amnesia, I tried hypnosis and at once the amnesia yielded; the dissociative barrier was overcome, and he continued in the waking state to be able to recollect and describe the whole incident: how a shell exploded near him, throwing him down; how he remounted his cycle and set off for the seaport; how he found his way by studying the signposts and asking questions, etc. It was clear that, though his actions had been conscious, intelligent and purposive, yet his conscious activity was of a restricted kind; he seemed to have had no thought about the consequences of his action, but to have been driven on by the single strong impulse of fear, taking the form of a desire to get far away from the danger-zone."

The above cases of so-called fugue typify a mental

---

[2] *Outline of Abnormal Psychology,* 258.

disease called *hysteria*. The malady is rather common, both among women and men, and takes countless forms, difficult to classify. Like other neuroses, hysteria is often left without medical attention and treatment, and only the graver cases are hospitalized. The ailment is of particular interest to us, because it manifests symptoms which, in many respects, parallel the phenomena of hypnosis. It is the consensus of medical opinion that hysteria *is not* caused by an organic trouble; at least, the latter could not be detected. Yet the patient may be totally or partially blind or deaf, be afflicted with the paralysis of limbs or side, suffer from fits, chorea or skin anaesthesia; or he may be a sleep-walker. Such a condition is serious enough to make any person desperate, it seems; yet surprisingly, despite the gravity of his trouble, the patient often feels no mental agonies whatever, but accepts the ailment indifferently, almost willingly. Now, the situation is quite paradoxical. Since hysteria is not caused by an organic deficiency (according to the nature of the trouble), there seems to be nothing to cure in the body. Yet the disease might lift by itself, if the patient's emotions are aroused to a high pitch, if he comes in contact with something inspiring his faith, or if he meets somebody commanding a high prestige in his eyes. Faith-healers and Christian Scientists have been quite successful in their evangelistic practice, not because they know the nature of their powerful influence, but because they provide the prestige supplying hysterics with the faith required to relieve them. An exceptional environment, such as found in Lourdes, France, where numerous "miracles" are recorded, may offer even a better opportunity for cure. That this power of alleviating pains and ailments does not proceed, however, from an external source but depends on some organic factors becomes fairly evident as we consider cases in which no suggestion is involved. We have all read, for example, of paralytics who start walking again in an emergency such as fire.

There is some foundation for describing hysteria as "unconscious pretense." For it reminds us of truant children who play sick to stay away from the school. But the child usually knows he pretends; the hysteric does not.

Take the following type of hysteria (technically designated as astasia-abasia), as described by Pierre Janet:[3] "The subjects are, as a rule, young people; they seem not to have the least paralysis of the legs, when you examine them in their bed. Not only are the reflexes intact, but—and the fact is more surprising—the movements are intact. If you tell them to raise their legs, to bend, to turn them, they do exactly all that is required of them. What is more, they have kept a very great strength, quite the normal strength. They push back your hand with their feet, they lift you up if you bear down with all your strength on their knees. Then, you will no doubt say, there is nothing at all the matter with them. It is true, but they are absolutely incapable of walking. If you cause them to stand on the floor, they will bend, twist their legs, throw them to one side and the other, and fall down without having made one step: and this will last for weeks and months. They realize the paradox of having no paralysis of the legs and of being unable to walk. In a few, described by

[3] *The Major Symptoms of Hysteria,* ed. 1920. p. 177.

Charcot, the comedy is still more complete; they are able to make with their legs certain movements which seem very complicated, as jumping, dancing, hopping on one leg, running, but they fall as soon as they try to walk. Can you conceive such an absurdity?"

This "unconscious pretense" of the hysterics—the pretense that they are gravely sick or badly crippled when they actually are not—seems to be even more obvious when you consider the cases of "limited vision." As Janet says,[4] "nothing is so inconvenient as a real contraction of the visual field (the extent of the surface an eye can see simultaneously, without moving); you know how the unfortunate people who are affected with chronic glaucoma complain of being no longer able to glance over their newspaper because they see only one word or one syllable at a time. Hysterics, on the other hand, who have an exceedingly small visual field, run without in the least troubling themselves about it. This is a curious fact to which I remember having attracted the attention of Charcot, who had not remarked it, and was very much surprised at it. I showed him two of our young patients playing very cleverly at ball in the court-yard of La Salpêtrière. Then, having brought them before him, I remarked to him that their visual field was reduced to a point, and I asked him whether he would be capable of playing at ball, if he had before each eye a card merely pierced with a small hole."

Another investigator reports the following curious case.[5] "A young girl, aged 15, with a marked neuro-pathic family history, had a sister who hurt her foot so

---

[4] *Ibid.,* 197-98.
[5] S. A. K. Wilson, "Some Modern French Conceptions of Hysteria," *Brain,* XXXIII (1911).

that it turned inwards. The patient unconsciously copied this, and when her attention was drawn to what she was doing, the contracture became worse; the toes were contracted and immovable, but found to be quite pliable during sleep. At the same time, wishing 'to be coddled', 'to be laid up for a little while', like her sister, she drove a large carpet tack into her right foot, but cannot remember whether it was painful or not. The foot became septic, and all sorts of complications ensued, but complete recovery eventually followed.

"When aged 19, in order to make the mistress of the school, of whom she was passionately fond, love her more, she cut the back of her left hand with glass. It was not particularly painful. 'I cut my glove, too, and pretended that I had been run into by a man carrying a frame of glass'.

"The next year, her mother being ill and in bed, the patient wanted to lie down, too, and 'be made a fuss of'. She therefore conceived the idea 'it would be nice to have spinal disease'. After waiting some weeks she procured some nitric acid, dipped a spun glass brush into it, and rubbed it up and down her back one evening. The back at once blistered and was exceedingly painful, but she had a quantity of white lead ready, and this she rubbed into her back as well as she could. When she could bear the pain no longer, she gave in, and was put under treatment at once, at the same time developing typical hysterical crises."

As in the above case, conscious and unconscious pretense may be combined or blended in the patient. But, in spite of all suspicions that we might entertain on learning the facts of a particular case, hysteria is never merely a deliberate pretense. There is no hysteria

apart from real bodily difficulties or defects, which are
not subject in any way to conscious control. The patient
may be puzzled by the strangeness of his case; or he
may sincerely believe himself to be organically sick.
The fact is that he usually is no more aware of the
cause of his malady than his relatives and friends. Why
then does he hurt himself? Why doesn't he use his
healthy organs and limbs? Why does his organism
refuse to obey his will when nothing is the matter with
it?

I concur with J. F. Babinski[6] in his conviction that
hysteria is a state of abnormal suggestibility. It is
generally acknowledged, indeed, that people suffering
from this disease react vigorously to outside influences.
They are easily carried away by ideas uttered in their
presence, they let imagination break the boundaries of
the common sense, they are led with facility to the ex-
tremes of emotionality. If we are to understand the
neurosis of hysteria, however, it is necessary to go
beyond the simple assertion that hysterics are exces-
sively suggestible. For it is not enough to grant that
hysteria is closely associated with suggestibility or
merely to define it as a pathological state of suggestibility. After all, what is the bodily mechanism underlying those after-effects of suggestion, which are separated, as in hysterical or hypnotized persons, from
conscious regulation?

Suggestion, it is true, is sometimes experienced consciously, and one is more or less distinctly aware of its
workings. It has to be experienced to start with—
seen or heard, sometimes even understood. On the

"My Conception of Hysteria and Hypnotism," *Alienist and Neurol-
ogist*, 1908. No. 1.

psychological side, therefore, the phenomenon is controlled largely by the central nervous system. But then
the suggestion is passed on. It becomes a physiological
phenomenon, or a way to reach the autonomic nervous
system, with resulting actions taking place apparently
with no control of conscious will. The hysterics are
suggestible in the latter sense. Suggestion works
physiologically rather than psychologically in them.
Their "pretense" is not willed at all.

Hysteria manifests itself either as the result of a
powerful emotion (fear, rage, love, religious ecstasy,
etc.) or as a consequence of the relationship of suggestion. It is cured, too, through emotion or suggestion.
What is even more interesting, *the symptoms of
hysteria can be removed by hypnosis*—which fact induced Charcot to believe that only neurotics, and particularly hysterics, can be hypnotized. Science owes a
great debt to Charcot for his observation that paralyses
and contractures, undistinguishable from those occur-
ring in hysteria, can also be produced by hypnotic
suggestion. As S. Freud, erstwhile Charcot's pupil,
said,[7] "such artificial products showed, down to their
smallest details, the same features as spontaneous
attacks." H. Bernheim subsequently demonstrated
that Charcot was wrong and that all people, not only
hysterics, can be hypnotized. Charcot himself was hard
to persuade, and before he was defeated, he made the
controversy one of the most colorful in the history of
European medicine.

By this time, clinical evidence is sufficiently rich and
complete to regard as firmly established the conclusion

---

[7] *Autobiography,* 19.

that, as F. W. H. Myers worded it, "not indeed all, but almost all, the phenomena which can be induced by suggestion in the hypnotic state occur spontaneously in hysterical patients." Full identity is out of question between the two sets of phenomena, hysteric and hypnotic. But the relationship is doubtless close. How can it be explained?

A similarity of effects, anywhere in nature, can be accounted for, barring accident, in one of two ways: either the phenomena in question are themselves of the same kind or they proceed from a common source. The first alternative having been disproved by Bernheim, it remains for us to accept the second. As a parallel study of the phenomena of suggestion (including hypnosis) and those of hysteria shows a remarkable functional similarity, it must be rooted in the *identity of the bodily mechanism* underlying them, that is to say, in the mechanism of the autonomic nervous system. Hysteria, like the hypnotic state, manifests the signs of both the excitatory and inhibitory functions of the autonomic nervous system. The precipitating cause of neurosis is, as clinical observation demonstrates, almost invariably some shock of personal experience, but the basic explanation is to be looked for in some functional or organic disorder of the autonomic nervous system.

There is, however, one important difference between hysteria and the hypnotic state, which accounts for the fact that people free from hysteria can nevertheless be hypnotized. Hysteria, namely, is a *disease,* a combination of *pathological* phenomena, indicating some defect of the system (glandular or neural), some unfortunate emotional experience in the patient's past (accident, love affair, bankruptcy, etc.), harmful influences of an unfriendly social environment (resulting in frustration and repression of basic urges, in unfavorable conditioned reflexes), or, most likely, some combination of these factors. All forms of hysteria, grave or mild, are symptoms of malady.

The hypnotic state, on the other hand, utilizes the *normal* mechanism of suggestion. A trance can be induced perhaps with greater ease among hysterics. Yet it is a mechanism found in all people, sick and healthy. Among normal people, to be sure, it does not manifest itself conspicuously, apart from hypnosis, and attracts one's attention no more than do the activities of one's liver or kidneys in a healthy condition. This mechanism is of great interest to the scientist, not only because it throws a new light on hysteria and, as we presently shall see, on psychoanalysis, Christian Science, and other forms of faith-healing, but also because a practical acquaintance with the physiology of suggestion opens countless other opportunities. Of that anon.

CHAPTER IV

PSYCHOANALYSIS AND SUGGESTION

The problem of hypnosis is much clarified, when we realize that the mechanism determining it accounts not only for the pathology of suggestibility (hysteria), but also for many old and current methods of treatment and cure of neurotic states, namely, for the practical successes of primitive faith-healing, of Christian Science, and of psychoanalysis. These three ways of handling mental diseases, though thoroughly unlike in assumptions, are identical in so far as they dress their doctrine in an obscure or mystical terminology and, especially, in so far as they command, and rest upon, the same bodily powers. The scientific approach to our problems demands that the latter dependence be revealed and insists on explaining all phenomena as natural.

The objective of this chapter is to discuss psychoanalysis, to demonstrate that its terminology and conceptology are pseudo-scientific, and to show that its practices and explanations presuppose the mechanism of the autonomic nervous system. My intention is, in other words, to demonstrate that, whereas some practical successes of psychoanalysis (as also those of faith-healing) cannot be denied, the theory underlying it is fallacious.

According to Freud and his fashionable followers, conscious experience, or contents of the mind at work, is but a small part of man's psychic life. "The Unconscious is the larger circle which includes the smaller circle of the Conscious; everything conscious has a preliminary unconscious stage, whereas the unconscious can stop at this stage, and yet claim to be considered a full psychic function. The Unconscious is the true psychic reality; in its inner nature it is just as much unknown as the reality of the external world, and it is just as imperfectly communicated to us by the data of consciousness as is the external world by the reports of our sense-organs."[1]

The Unconscious, not being conscious and not being open to direct observation, can be known only indirectly, by its consequences. The assumption is fairly plausible, at a first glance. For is it not true that many actions are performed as it were on the margin of awareness or even quite automatically? Is it not true that all perceptions and thoughts disappear from consciousness, but many of them re-appear from somewhere (we call it memory)? Sigmund Freud invokes this reservoir of hidden experience to explain (so he contends) much of pathological and normal behavior and to cure a variety of neuroses. Let us, therefore, see precisely what the assumptions of psychoanalysis are.

Man is a being of countless urges, among which the sex impulse plays a very important role. Until recently, false shame and prejudices stood in the way of recognizing this obvious fact. It used to be improper to discuss the problem of sex in decent company, especially

---

[1] S. Freud, *The Interpretation of Dreams* (translated by A. A. Brill). Ed. 1933, p. 562. A similar theory was entertained by F. W. H. Myers, who distinguished between the "subliminal" and "superliminal" consciousness.

if women and girls (heavens!) were present. Even the scientists carefully avoided the topic, except in the language of esoteric learning. However, the development of anatomy, physiology, and hygiene made difficult the continuance of this ridiculous attitude. Toward the end of the last century prudery began to recede, perhaps because religious sanctions weakened, and serious men commenced to comprehend the universality and dominance of the sex impulse. Freud was the first scholar to raise the entire problem to the level of open and popular discussion. In W. B. Wolfe's words,[2] "Freud found sex an outcast in the outhouse, and he left it in the living room, an honored guest. For this he deserves the eternal gratitude of all men."

The basic doctrine of psychoanalysis is that "libido," the fountain of sex desire, motivates and directs practically all human activity. Not only that of adults, mind you, but also that of small children. For, in Freud's interpretation, the sex impulse assumes many forms, overt and covert, including "love" and "tenderness." In Freud's own words, "the most remarkable feature of the sexual life of man is that it comes on in two waves, with an interval between them. It reaches a first maximum in the fourth or fifth year of a child's life. But this early growth of sexuality is nipped in the bud; the sexual impulses which have shown such liveliness are overcome by repression, and a period of latency follows, which lasts until puberty."[3]

In this world of ours, no person can live as he pleases and find complete satisfaction of bodily appetites and

---

[2] "The Twilight of Psychoanalysis," *The American Mercury*, August, 1935.
[3] *Autobiography*, 70.

mental desires.   He is submerged in a social environment that is essentially competitive, regulated by laws, customs, and fashions preventing people from being fully free.   As a result, human wishes often fail to be realized, leaving in one's mind the feeling of dissatisfaction or frustration.   Though it is possible to adjust oneself to these social conditions, nevertheless wishes barred from fulfillment commonly persist and struggle for realization within the mind.   Borrowing this idea from Herbart, Freud believes that experiences are forces, deriving their power from sex impulses and related bodily urges.

Repressions are everyday occurrences.   But they are seldom accepted without a struggle: one has to be badly broken in spirit, to submit consistently to the blows of life.   If no effort avails, man will usually seek some sort of substitute. His desires may find a vicarious realization in day or night dreams, taking a symbolic form of which the psychoanalyst is a clever (too clever) interpreter.   Or man's energies may be sublimated, finding an outlet in sentimental poetry, in the pursuit of scientific knowledge, in a business career, or in whatever he finds the satisfaction of his emotional inclinations, of his ambition and vanity.

It is well if frustrated desires—and who is free from them?—find some direct or vicarious compensation. In many instances, the feeling of defeat presses heavily on the mind, disturbing one's life, distorting one's personality, driving one into abnormal satisfaction of sexual appetite, or resulting in some mental disease. These people have to be helped, for they are sick. Drugs and medicine in general are of small use in this respect.   The cure neurotics need is psychological. And the school of psychoanalysis claims to have found a method of relieving people from repressions and complexes.

The psychoanalytic treatment is quite simple in principle. First, the psychoanalyst urges the patient to talk, to tell of his past experience and recent impressions, to complain, to confess his urges and emotions (the procedure is known as "catharsis"). "The physician listens, tries to direct the thought processes of the patient, reminds him of things, forces his attention into certain channels, gives him explanations and observes the reactions of understanding or denial which he calls forth in the patient."[4] This confession of long suppressed wishes alone may help the neurotic. But the psychoanalyst is not satisfied with this passive role. While listening to his client or giving him various tasks to perform, he watches closely for clues to some forgotten experience that may have precipitated the pathological development of his patient's personality. Especially important are, according to Freud, clues derived from dreams. The psychoanalyst regards it as his duty to investigate these. To assist such analysis, the celebrated Viennese physician has devised a manual of dream interpretation, in which we find lengthy lists of symbols of night life. Witness some of them:

"A particularly remarkable dream symbol is that of having one's teeth fall out, of having them pulled. Certainly (sic!) its most immediate interpretation is castration as a punishment for onanism."[5]

"Parents appear in the dream as *king* and *queen*, or

---

[4] S. Freud, *A General Introduction to Psychoanalysis* (translated by G. S. Hall). Ed. 1920. p. 1.
[5] *Ibid.,* 129.

other persons highly respected. The dream in this instance is very pious. It treats children, and brothers and sisters, less tenderly; they are symbolized as *little animals* or *vermin*. Birth is almost regularly represented by some reference to *water*. . .

"The more conspicuous and more interesting part of the genital to both sexes, the male organ, has symbolical substitute in objects of like form, those which are long and upright, such as *sticks, umbrellas, poles, trees,* etc. It is also symbolized by objects that have the characteristic, in common with it, of penetration into the body and consequent injury, hence pointed *weapons* of every type, *knives, daggers, lances, swords,* and in the same manner *firearms, guns, pistols* and the *revolver,* which is so suitable because of its shape. . . Easily comprehensible, too, is the substitution for the male member of objects out of which water flows: *faucet, water cans, fountains,* as well as its representation by other objects that have the power of elongation, such as hanging *lamps, collapsible pencils,* etc. That *pencils, quills, nail files, hammers* and other *instruments* are undoubtedly (sic!) male symbols is a fact connected with a conception of the organ, which likewise is not far to seek.

"The extraordinary characteristic of the member of being able to raise itself against the force of gravity, one of the phenomena of erection, leads to symbolic representations of *balloons, aeroplanes,* and more recently, *Zeppelins.* The dream has another far more expressive way of symbolizing erection. It makes the sex organ the essential part of the whole person and pictures the person himself as *flying.* . .

"To the less comprehensible male sex-symbols belong

certain *reptiles* and *fish,* notably the famous symbol of the *snake.* Why *hats* and *cloaks* should have turned to the same use is certainly difficult to discover, but their symbolic meaning leaves no room for doubt (sic!)."[6]

Professor Freud continues in this fashion, sparkling with his imagination and giving impressive lists as to how the female genitals, the breasts, etc., are represented in dreams. No wonder that a psychoanalyst, armed with this impressive array of symbols, is able to interpret every dream as fundamentally sexual in nature!

If we are to believe Freud, the reason why dreams and other experiences due to frustration of natural urges take such a strange symbolic form is that the mechanism of the Unconscious has a special device called "the censor," standing at the gateway to the Conscious and forbidding repressed wishes and ideas to enter the field of mental awareness, except in a careful disguise exemplified by dream symbols. Believe it or not!

Far be it from me to deny the importance of all the contributions of the psychoanalysts. No one can take away from Freud his historical place in the development of modern psychology. His emphasis on sex is the stress of our days, though the real reason for it is not so much the "instinct" as the changed social and economic conditions playing havoc with biological urges. Nor can we disregard the contributions of his most renowned disciples, now heretics of the movement. Mr. Jung's classification of personalities (introverts and extraverts) is as instructive and significant as Hip-

---

[6] *Ibid.,* 125-128.

pocrates' ancient classification of temperaments. Mr. Adler's individual psychology, with its study of struggles and defeats of men in their social environment, is fraught with most remarkable insights. Psychoanalysts' explanations and findings are, in general, quite ingenious, their observations are commonly clever and acute, and their clinical records are a mine of precious information. But their theories—let me be perfectly frank—savor of the fantastic if not of the mystical. The "Unconscious," "libido," "censor" and, more recently, the triad of the "id," "ego" and "super-ego," in short their entire terminology, are a collection of figurative if not occult names. The leading psychoanalysts' observations constitute, as remarked by L. Granich,[7] "a brilliant contribution; their fantastic hypotheses are an obstacle to scientific progress. . . It is a notorious fact that the laws and generalizations of psychoanalysis have been issued by a few men in the manner of prophets, and have been accepted on pure faith. We cannot accept as omniscient, or reliable, individuals whose pronouncements have often shown incredible naiveté."

In the post-war years, scholars began to overcome their strange curiosity and devotion in regard to psychoanalysis. The movement's pseudo-scientific jargon no longer could satisfy the real scientist. The vague flexibility of doctrines attracted charlatans and, consequently, repelled serious-minded people. This situation cannot continue much longer. "It is time," urges G. Humphrey,[8] "for a revision of the Freudian conception

---

[7] "A Systematic Translation of Psychoanalytic Concepts," the *Journal of Abnormal and Social Psychology*, 1932.
[8] "Education and Freudianism," *The Journal of Abnormal Psychology*, 1920-21.

of the Unconscious." "The crisis of psychoanalysis is at hand," contends J. Jastrow,[9] "the critical stage in its appraisal will presently be in full tide." Elsewhere the same author advises "to correct one false notion, and do it as curtly as that brief essay on the Snakes of Ireland, which said: 'There are no snakes in Ireland'. There is no subconscious mind!"[10] In other words, though many neural phenomena are not conscious, there is no independent entity which can be identified with the Unconscious.

The central fault of the psychoanalytic theory is easily located. The protagonists of the movement contend that all mental deviations from the normal, particularly neuroses (even psychoses), must be explained functionally, that is to say, as resulting from shocks of experience, from the repression and frustration of natural urges and desires. But a growing number of psychiatrists and psychologists now looks askance at the loose and arbitrary language of the psychoanalysts. They point out that the term "function" serves to conceal rather than to reveal the explanation of mental disorders, which have to be ultimately accounted for in physiological terms. Practically the same can be said of other psychoanalytic concepts. "It has always seemed to me," says E. J. Kempf,[11] "that the inability of earnest, intelligent students of medicine and psychology to grasp Freud's and Jung's libido concepts indicates that there must be something not quite satisfactory with the idea of libido."

No doubt, many ailments, physical and mental,

[9] The House that Freud Built, 261.
[10] Sanity First, 1935. p. 86.
[11] The Autonomic Function and the Personality: Nervous and Mental Disease Monograph Series, No. 28. p. vii.

originate in emotional experiences. But one should not forget that emotion is no less a physiological than a psychological phenomenon. And whatever changes occur in the organism as a result of emotion, they are due to its physiological aspect. The ultimate basis of all disorders resides in the body. The entire field of psychological phenomena, including lapses of memory, excesses of imagination, tricks of emotion, etc., must depend on some organic processes taking place often in the nervous system itself. Our ignorance of organic processes is still stupendous, yet the search for understanding points definitely in that direction. Why Freud, in his youth (1883-84) himself a student of brain functions, and particularly of those of medulla oblongata, should have failed to avail himself of a physiological interpretation of his theories is, indeed, strange. One senses life's irony in Freud's own acknowledgement that in the last analysis psychoanalysis must be established on the organic foundations.

The emphasis on the functional interpretation of human psychology would have been more comprehensible, did Freud derive his theories from the consideration that repressions and neuroses find their origin in the inadequacies of our social system, and especially in the inadequacies of our institutions of marriage and the family. But no. Freud disregards economic problems and social psychology almost to the same extent to which he neglects physiology. He passes without due consideration even the phenomenon which, of all people, should have attracted his attention; namely, that, in our urban civilization, young men and women get married many years after they have reached biological maturity, usually because they cannot afford to assume the economic responsibilities connected with family life. And yet Freud believes himself to be a profound interpreter of sex problems!

If psychoanalysis is to survive as a theoretical and practical movement, its leaders must comprehend the dependence of human experience upon economic factors and social institutions. Above all, they must learn to translate their contentions into terms of bodily responses and to modify their theories in accordance with scientific data and discoveries. As long as they refuse or fail to take this attitude, they will be unable to meet the criticism of such men as K. S. Lashley who said:[12] "The psychoanalysts have developed a crude mechanistic system of explanation based upon analogy with simple physical forces and with complete disregard of physiological facts which bear directly upon their problems. Their explanations, in so far as they are based upon the conception of physical or vital energy, are flatly contradicted by physiological evidence." Another noted critic sharply maintains:[13] "Psychoanalysts must come within the fold of psychology or risk the fate of estrangement from the currents of progress."

Among the most outspoken and vigorous critics of psychoanalysis is Dr. Milton Harrington. He is right in asserting that "psychoanalysis is not a stranger who has come among us and has risen to sudden eminence; but an old and ever popular friend who merely put on a new dress."[14] Basically, it is a kind of treatment used by witch doctors long before the birth of modern medi-

---

[12] "Physiological Analysis of the Libido," *The Psychological Review*, 1924.
[13] J. Jastrow, *The House that Freud Built*, 285.
[14] *Wish-Hunting in the Unconscious*, 1934. p. 125.

cine. The great success of psychoanalysis never lay primarily among the scientists, but among the semi-educated seekers of the sensational. And Freud's admirers come mainly from among those who themselves suffer from various complexes, repressions and defense mechanisms. For mental patients are driven to Freudian theories and practices by the same power which directs so many people like them to Lourdes, France, and to the temples of Christian Science. This power is nothing other than hope for relief, consolation, and for the justification of one's beliefs.

As far as the medical men who have become enthusiastic converts to Freudianism are concerned, they are attracted to psychoanalysis because it "is, among other things, a great face-saving device. It saves all those who embrace it from the humiliation and embarrassment of having to admit ignorance. It renders them wise in their own eyes and in the eyes of their disciples."[15] Freud's technique has given our contemporaries, indeed, "a device by means of which anyone can find practically any wish he chooses to look for, lying back of any symptom he chooses to explain, even although there is no wish of any sort there to find."[16] M. A. May holds practically the same opinion:[17] "There is truly no form of human behavior and no event in history that the agile psychoanalyst cannot explain by the simple process of selecting from his list a few explanatory terms that fit the case. The fallacy of explaining a complicated process by giving it a

---

[15] *Ibid.,* 123.
[16] *Ibid.,* 117.
[17] "The Foundation of Personality," in *Psychology at Work* (Symposium), 94.

name, and thereby setting at ease the mind of the in-
quirer, is very common in psychoanalysis."

Dr. H. T. Hyman points out a distinct bias as well as
the lack of scientific objectivity in the works of Freud's
followers. "There have appeared," he says,[18] "an
abundance of abstract discussions of life and death,
war and peace, politics and criminology, art and letters,
education and pedagogy, love and hate, wit and humor,
the conscious and the unconscious. But analyses of
individual case histories, reports of failures, confes-
sions of limitations, end results after a lapse of a
reasonable span of time, allowances for the spontaneous
course of disease (as in the manic-depressive psychoses), considerations of external factors such as arise
in the life circumstances of any individual, attempts to
adjudge the value of the results in terms of the time
and money consumed—all these are conspicuously
absent from the writings of men and women whose life
work is devoted to the study and teachings of in-
tegrated correlation."

With complete disregard of the concrete realities of
the human organism and of social conditions, driven by
the temptations of loose language and thought, Freud
built his system upon the stupendous assumption that
what we used to regard as distortions of the mind is
really man's true nature. "So the normal mind is made
over into the image of a Freudian neurosis; every baby,
the psychoanalyst discovers, is a sexual pervert."[19]

Dr. Harrington's criticism may appear unduly sharp,
but a scholar with scientific training will have to accept

---

[18] "The Value of Psychoanalysis as a Therapeutic Procedure," the
Journal of American Medical Association, August 1, 1936.
[19] *Wish-Hunting in the Unconscious,* 133.

it. Every word he utters is backed by facts and sound reasoning, amounting simply to a scientist's demand that the study of natural phenomena be free from the elements of fancy. His position is further strengthened by a repeated discrimination between the psychoanalytic theory and its practice. But even in the latter he finds few merits. It cannot be denied, of course, that the psychoanalysts do succeed in helping quite a few patients, perhaps because there are so many hysterics among them, who can best be cured by faith anyway and by persons of prestige who are rumored to be in possession of exceptional curative powers. "When we come to look at psychoanalysis from the standpoint of its practical value in the prevention and cure of mental disorder, we find that here also there is very little to be said in its favor. Psychoanalysis gives us no mental hygiene, no treatment for the psychoses. All it gives us is a new treatment for the neuroses, which is apparently just a new form of suggestion therapy."[20]

Mystical approach remains the most insiduous fault of psychoanalysis, from the scientific standpoint. It "attempts to explain abnormal behavior without taking into consideration the anatomical mechanism by which all behavior, both normal and abnormal, is produced. The psychoanalyst is like a physician who would explain heart disease without so much as recognizing the existence of the heart and blood vessels."[21]

There is, however, no smoke without fire, as the saying goes. Suggestion-therapy, whether it be psycho-

---

[20] *Ibid.*, 119.
[21] *Ibid.*, 134. Among the distinguished critics of psychoanalysis, we find, in addition to those mentioned in the text, A. Wohlgemuth, R. S. Woodworth, H. L. Hollingworth, and K. Dunlap.

analysis, Christian Science, or faith-healing, is not without foundation. The phenomena with which all three deal must be in some sense real, for otherwise whence the results? Psychoanalytic cures are often real, too, and for the same reason that faith-healing was practically successful in the days of our ignorant ancestors, absurd as it was in its assumptions and explanations. Freud's hypotheses are too crude to be accepted. But what interpretation can take its place? What views will reconcile factual accomplishments of psychoanalysis with science?

Freud, we may recall, was originally a student of Charcot. He studied and practised hypnotism, and his patients were often hysterics. But he did not quite fit into the shoes of his teacher and found waking suggestion much more to his taste. Taking up Breuer's hint, he devised the rules of psychoanalysis as a better substitute (so he believed) for other methods of suggestion treatment. His approach was thoroughly practical and, coupled with the vast imagination he possessed, led him away from, rather than toward, the study of causes, which underlies all science. Now, suggestion does not operate *in vacuo,* but in a human body; and its effects arise not as a result of "telepathy," but through the mediation of a bodily mechanism. This mechanism, we must remind ourselves, is active in every sort of prestige-and-faith situation and is nothing other than *the autonomic nervous system,* connected in both directions with the central nervous system and, through it, with conscious experience.

The basic operations of the human body have been but slightly modified by civilization. Our conscious activities and what we call education may provide us with a wealth of knowledge and with a brilliant gloss of good manners. Our machines, roads, towns, institutions and customs, in short, our entire social environment, may stimulate us to behavior that is characteristic of modern culture. But beneath this superficial accruement, there lies animal nature, hardly changed since the days of the Neanderthal Man. There is nothing intellectual or refined about it. It is nature in the raw. It demands food and water, proper temperature, and sex satisfaction. Moral and aesthetic consideration are totally foreign to the human body. Is it then surprising that, when the psychoanalysts reach for the animal within the man and find the "Unconscious" (or the "id"), really a mystic symbol of the autonomic nervous system, they describe it as primitive, brutal, infantile? Of course, the body and the nervous system regulating it are primitive. They date from the very dawn of life. And when consciousness is blinded or choked, leaving action to bodily impulses alone, what can they be but brutal? Even the word "infantile" is suitable to describe the behavior arising from the autonomic nervous system. For, of all the human beings, only new born children are perfect animals. But the psychoanalysts, it seems, cannot see facts assigned to their proper places and called by their right names. Freud and his followers evidently derive great pleasure from shuffling facts, inventing fantastic entities, and supplying profuse mystery, lest somebody recognizes truths for what they are.

Inhibition, as one of the functions of the involuntary nervous system, accounts for many other phenomena, for the explanation of which Freud has created unnecessary and obscure concepts and terms. There is no need, for instance, to resort to "libido" to comprehend the importance of sex impulses, to invoke the "Unconscious" to explain the simple fact of forgetting or even complex symptoms of hysteria, and to bring into existence a "censor" to see that inhibitions commonly persist. Even the word "repression" is superfluous, unless it be recognized as synonymous with "inhibition."

Here, then, is the way toward the solution of an old problem. Within the human organism, there lies a nervous system which controls and regulates the mechanical behavior of the body. Involuntary as it usually is, it is not entirely separated from consciousness. The autonomic system is connected with the central system by means of two channels, emotion and suggestion. It was the pathway of suggestion—ornamented with prejudice and superstition—that was unwittingly exploited from the olden days to the present, from the witch-doctors to the psychoanalysts. Whereas they failed to comprehend the physical mechanism of suggestion and ascribed their powers to the spirits or by whatever other names these forces were called, it is time now to abandon the antiquated attitude and to seek the explanation of phenomena of suggestion within the organism itself—that is to say, to study functions of the autonomic nervous system and structures connected with it. When we finally learn to understand this mechanism in its major details, we shall be enabled to treat human beings not at random and through guesses, but scientifically, with all that this word implies.

CHAPTER V

WHAT IS THE HYPNOTIC STATE?

It was James Braid (1795–1861) who both destroyed the superstition of "animal magnetism" and constructed the preliminary foundations of scientific hypnotism. He demonstrated, namely, that no invisible "fluid" passes between the practician and his subject in trance, and that the entire phenomenon depends simply on suggestion. Nothing illustrates this achievement better than the following incident related by Bramwell:[1] "One day Braid called on a London physician who used mesmerism in his practice. The latter told him that he had been obtaining wonderful results from the use of magnets, and offered to demonstrate this on a subject who was at that moment in a state of mesmeric trance. He asserted, for example, that when he touched the subject's limbs with the magnet, this produced catalepsy; and, certainly, what he had predicted, happened. Braid, in his turn, stated that he had an instrument in his pocket which was quite as powerful, and offered to prove this by operating on the same subject. He then informed the doctor, in the subject's presence, that when he put the instrument into her hands it would produce catalepsy; and it at once did so, just as in the former instance. Having terminated the catalepsy by means of passes, Braid placed the instrument in another position, and stated that it would now have

[1] *Hypnotism*, 287.

the very reverse effect—that the subject would not be able to hold it, owing to paralysis of her muscles: this, as well as many other experiments, was successful. Braid then privately explained to the doctor the real nature and powers of his apparently magical instrument. It was nothing more than his portmanteau-key and ring, and its varied powers were merely the result of the predictions which the subject had heard Braid make. The experiments, he said, simply illustrated the power of suggestion during hypnosis: neither magnet nor portmanteau-key played any real part in them."

Mesmerism, in its original form, has long been dead. However, every once in a while some scholar attempts to resuscitate the notion of "animal magnetism," though the phrase itself is no longer used. Only recently S. Alrutz and G. Wallenius propounded the theory of "nervous effluence" and that of "nervous radiation." Fortunately, few intelligent people took these views seriously. But then again, the belief in some substances or rays passing between two minds, unfounded as it is, might come back. Superstitions, it seems, have many lives. I shall not be surprised if the next form of mesmerism will be connected with "telepathy," which intrigues today many an ignorant and mystical mind.

For the time being, however, mesmerism is dead. But in its place, there arose other dangerous notions which detracted scientific attention from more tenable explanations of suggestion and hypnosis. Charcot and his Salpêtrière School, assuming that the trance is nothing but a state of artificial hysteria, have created the unfortunate concept of "mental dissociation." In this view, the mind can be divided into two (or more) practically independent parts and function as such, though only one will command consciousness at a time. Today this concept of dissociation is being used in a variety of ways and under the guise of erudite language, as when it is said: "Hypnosis may best be characterized as a phenomenon entailing a splitting of consciousness in which the simultaneous and successive nexus of mental life is partially deranged."[2] I have read many a modern book on psychology but, heaven knows, I have not yet discovered what such phrases really mean. The idea of "split" and "divided" personality was made fashionable by striking studies of Morton Prince (particularly, in connection with the famous case of Miss Beauchamp), and further popularized by the psychoanalytic theory of the Unconscious. So-called "shell-shocks" of the war-time and hysterical amnesias seemed only to confirm this interpretation. And numerous psychiatrists succumbed to the temptation of fashionable theories and resorted to them to explain the phenomena of hypnosis. Witness, for instance, the following interpretation of what happens during the trance: "You are in touch with the unconscious mind of the subject, which is just as capable of handling the body and is just as acute as is the individual's conscious mind. . . This simple technique puts you in touch with the unconscious mind of the subject, which explains (sic!) the spectacular results which are observed. First of all, this unconscious mind is extremely suggestible . . ."[3] What is it, mere naiveté?

How easily one succumbs to the apparent plausibility of such interpretation is obvious from the following

[2] R. Mueller-Freienfels, *The Evolution of Modern Psychology*, 362.
[3] G. H. Estabrooks, "Hypnotism," *Scientific American*, 1936.

case of "negative hallucination," as related with comments by W. McDougall:[4] "I place five new postage stamps upon a white card and ask B (a hypnotized Hindu subject) to count them, which he does correctly pointing his finger to each in turn. I then point to two of the stamps and tell him they will be no longer there when he again looks at the card. I then ask him to count the three stamps again, and he points to and counts the three stamps and denies that the others are there. I then shuffle the stamps, while hidden from his vision, and ask him to count again. In spite of the changes of position of the stamps, B. still neglects and denies the two tabooed stamps. This illustrates two points: first, that the two stamps are really in some sense perceived; secondly, that they are perceived and finely discriminated from the other three; for, if they were not thus perceived and discriminated, they could not be singled out for neglect. But nevertheless, the two stamps are, in some sense, really invisible to the subject.

"The paradox that the stamps are seen and yet not seen by the patient," concludes Professor McDougall, "can only be resolved by the hypothesis that he at the same time is a divided personality, one part of which sees the two stamps and prevents the other from seeing them." This supposition, so appealing to the mystic or the animist and so convenient for hasty interpretations, is devoid of scientific meaning, as it cannot be, or at least has never been, translated into physiological terminology. In absence of any alternative hypothesis, scientists may be forced to resort to it. But it is

---

[4] *Outline of Abnormal Psychology*, 92-93.

neither obvious nor necessary. As a matter of fact, we have established in preceding pages that the phenomena of hypnosis and hysteria as well as those studied by psychoanalysis, different as they all appear to be, have this in common: they all are largely rooted in activities of the autonomic nervous system. This system is primarily reflexive, controlling and regulating the bodily functions which require no cooperation of consciousness or intellect; yet it is not fully involuntary, as it is continually, almost constantly, influenced by two related types of experience, namely, by emotion and by suggestion. Clearly, McDougall's case can easily be accounted for as a result of inhibition, established and removed by means of verbal suggestion.

Though the mechanism of suggestion is one and the same in every case, phenomena produced through it do not always resemble one another. We should not forget that the autonomic nervous system controls every sort of involuntary action. Consequently, manifestations and effects of suggestion or auto-suggestion are so varied as to constitute a vast realm in their own right, so closely intertwined with the realm of voluntary experience—as in love, hope, or dreams—that the two realms can seldom be fully separated.

The behavior of a hysteric does not seem to be very much like the conduct of a person under hypnosis. Nor can a man suffering from a complex of inferiority be confused with one in a trance. Any one who has had but a single opportunity to witness a hypnotic session knows that a hypnotized person does not look like a man in the state of high suggestibility, such as one observes in the whims and passions of an excited mob or in the moods of a waking neurotic. It is customary to believe that people are most open to suggestion while they are wide awake. But a hypnotic, for all we see, does not seem to be wide awake. Rather, he looks as if he were asleep.

These two sets of facts—the indubitable evidence, on the one hand, that hypnotized people are under the strong influence of the practician, to the point of obeying even nonsensical commands of his, and the apparent truth, on the other, that the subject is in the stage ranging in depth from mere drowsiness to stupor—led many learned observers to conclude that hypnosis is a paradoxical phenomenon in which the state of high mental suggestibility is combined with bodily sleep.

At a first glance, hypnosis does resemble sleep. In both cases, the subject loses his waking tendency to spontaneous movement and independent thinking. Consciousness may disappear, totally or partially. But whenever experience is sufficiently clear and vivid in the trance, it carries realistic imagery, such as is found in dreams. The breathing is deep and slow. The muscles are usually relaxed.

Nothing is simpler than to conclude that both states are related if not identical. There were, indeed, few observers of note who thought otherwise. Bernheim expressly stated that "in ordinary sleep, as soon as waking consciousness recedes, the subject finds himself merely in relationship with himself. In suggested sleep his mind retains the awareness of the person who put him to sleep—hence the hypnotist's power of guiding his imagination, of suggesting dreams, and of directing his actions which are no longer controlled by the submerged will." More recently, A. Forel voiced this consensus of opinion, by saying:[5] "The relationship of hypnosis and sleep is unmistakable, and I agree with Liébeault when he says that the former is only distinguishable in its essence from the latter by the fact of the connection between the sleeper and the hypnotist."

This view is still further substantiated by the common experience of hypnotists that their subjects pass from the trance into the state of ordinary sleep. There are quite a few instances in my own practice, especially when dealing with large groups of students, when I found on my hands a person peacefully dozing or accompanying his slumber with an unmistakable snoring. "There is really nothing surprising or paradoxical," remarks C. L. Hull,[6] "about a subject passing into natural sleep while in the trance, particularly if his posture happens to be one favorable for sleep and he be left undisturbed. These conditions, together with the quiescence usually imposed on the subject by the suggestions, are exactly those which normally induce sleep. As a matter of fact, the transition from hypnosis into sleep and from sleep into the trance without an intervening waking interval has been repeatedly reported, though without accompanying objective evidences which are necessary to render interpretation unambiguous."

A certain similarity between sleep and the hypnotic state is fairly obvious. Nevertheless, there exist undeniable distinctions between them, noticed comparatively long ago, in the works of Hirsch and Lehmann. There is a phenomenon, for example, known to science

---

[5] *Hypnotism and Psychotherapy*, 1907. p. 69.
[6] *Hypnosis and Suggestibility*, 207.

since the days of "animal magnetism," which reminds us more of hysteria than of ordinary sleep. This is the state of utter rigidity, usually designated as "catalepsy," which comes spontaneously or can be induced by suggestion in the deeper forms of hypnosis. The power of what amounts to "paralyzing by suggestion" was most effectively used and abused in popular demonstrations of hypnosis; the more so, as muscular rigidity can often be induced with remarkable ease. Such power of the hypnotist over muscles of his subject was well and concisely described by Moll:[7]

"Muscular activity can nearly always be influenced in a high degree by suggestion. By means of it we can make movements impossible, or else induce movements. I can make the subject's arm powerless to move simply by arousing in her (him) the conviction that her (his) arm is powerless. In just the same way the movements of the legs, trunk, larynx, etc., escape the subject's notice. 'You cannot raise your arm; cannot put out your tongue'. This suffices to make the forbidden movement impossible. In some cases the inability to move arises because the person cannot voluntarily contract his muscles, and his arm consequently hangs limp; while in other cases a contracture of the antagonistic muscles makes every attempt at a voluntary movement useless. In the same manner the leg will lose the power of motion at command. The power of speech can be taken away. And it is even possible to allow the muscles to contract for one particular purpose only. If we say to a hypnotic subject, 'you can only say your own name; for the rest you are absolutely dumb', the desired effect

---

[7] *Hypnotism*, 70.

will be produced. In the same way it is possible to prevent movements of the arm for any particular purpose. Thus we can make it impossible for a person to write, though he will be able to do any other kind of work. The subject can sew, play the piano, etc., but all efforts to write are vain."

There exists other evidence showing a definite distinction between sleep and the hypnotic state, which easily escapes the attention of an untrained observer. Since appearances are often deceptive, it was important, for determining the exact nature of hypnosis, to apply some scientific test to processes within the body, particularly to the nervous system. Having selected reflex activity of the organism as such crucial test, M. J. Bass found that, whereas in sleep the knee-jerk is clearly inhibited, it shows "no differentiation between the normal waking state and the hypnotic trance... These results make it quite clear that the hypnotic trance can not be considered as having any more than a superficial resemblance to sleep. Physiologically we may assume that the states are quite different."[8] Drs. E. N. Harvey, G. Hobart and A. L. Loomis arrived at a similar conclusion in their study of the "brain-waves" (fluctuations in the electrical potential of the brain).

There is, therefore, no need for us to believe that sleep and hypnosis are strictly identical. Their apparent similarity may signify a certain kinship of the two kinds of phenomena, a kinship assumed by the practicians since the days of Braid who called the hypnotic state "a nervous and artificial sleep." The late Professor I. P. Pavlov was the leading champion of the

---

[8] "Differentiation of the Hypnotic Trance from Normal Sleep," *Journal of Experimental Psychology*, 1931.

hypothesis that ordinary sleep and hypnosis belong to the same group of phenomena and are merely different manifestations of inhibitory processes. According to him, the distinction between them can be briefly described as follows: "Inhibition is partial sleep, or sleep distributed in localized parts, forced into narrow limits. . . Hypnosis is inhibition spread over the usually active points in special areas of the hemispheres. Sleep is inhibition irradiated over the whole area of active points of the hemispheres and even over some parts of the brain below the cerebral hemispheres."[9]

I find myself in fairly close agreement with Pavlov, in so far as he recognized the neural origin of hypnosis and the vital role of inhibition in its inward and outward manifestations. However, neither Pavlov nor his predecessors have apparently noticed the important fact—or thought important to emphasize it—that the control and regulation of inhibition involved in hypnosis, and probably also in sleep, resides primarily in the autonomic nervous system and finds its expression, only as an effect, in the cortex of the brain, which is the seat of consciousness. As far as sleep is concerned, its lasting nature, with drowsiness commonly preceding and following it, seems to indicate a neural inhibition accompanied with general metabolic changes. It is possible that the latter are due to the secretion of substances like hypothetical "hypnotoxin" of Piéron or, more likely, "sympathin" of Cannon and Rosenblueth. The quickness with which inhibition and excitation set in and vanish in a hypnotic state, demonstrates that the

---

[9] "The Identity of Inhibition with Sleep and Hypnosis," *Scientific Monthly*, 1923.

changes constituting the bodily state of hypnosis are mainly of neural nature. Consequently, they can be introduced or removed with the speed of nervous conduction, that is to say, practically instantaneously.

The bodily aspect of hypnosis, we see, is fairly clear: it is essentially a state of neural inhibition (occasionally combined with the excitation of particular functions), as controlled by the autonomic nervous system. The scope and intensity of manifestations vary with the case, but invariably they are limited by the distribution of autonomic fibres and by their specific activities. Such fibres, we know, do not innervate every tissue; hence, there are bodily parts which cannot be reached by suggestion, not directly at least.

What makes hypnosis particularly interesting, however, is that the bodily mechanism underlying it can be directed by the conscious will of the hypnotist and, consequently, may be used for various medical, psychological and educational purposes. In this mental aspect hypnosis is a relationship between two or more persons, in which the subject or subjects, being in a state of high suggestibility, react to suggestion of the practician. This mental attitude of *prestige-and-faith* relationship has to be established before the trance is induced, but is maintained and further consolidated during the state and after its conclusion.

The term ordinarily used in this connection is "rapport." According to an old belief, rapport constitutes a special and necessary relationship, by virtue of which the subject responds exclusively to suggestions of the hypnotist. No other person supposedly can influence the subject, not during the trance at least. Rapport so understood is not, indeed, a rare phenomenon. Any practician remembers numerous cases in which the subject, easily reacting to his suggestions, remained completely deaf to the voices of other persons. Nevertheless, comparatively simple experimentation shows that, in many instances of light hypnosis, it is hardly noticeable at all. The subject, on being aroused from the state, will commonly report on what has been said by other persons during the experiment. He might even spontaneously react to their remarks. We must conclude, therefore, that, whereas the prestige-and-faith relationship is absolutely necessary for successful hypnotizing, rapport is merely a common concomitant. As a matter of fact, such was essentially the view of Braid who pointed out long ago that rapport is not a necessary condition of hypnosis, but is created by suggestion. This position was recently confirmed by P. C. Young and others. As E. S. Conklin briefly puts it, "rapport is but a form of partial anesthesia, the subject being limited in his sensory responses to those aroused by the hypnotizer."[10]

By combining both aspects of hypnosis, physiological and psychological, we arrive at the following definition of *the hypnotic state*: it *is a prestige-and-faith relationship in which the practician uses his advantageous position to influence by suggestion the subject's autonomic nervous system, in order to effect desired bodily inhibitions and excitations and to condition his mind accordingly.*

---

[10] *Principles of Abnormal Psychology*, ed. 1935. p. 334.

PART II

PRACTICE

CHAPTER VI

How to Hypnotize

A. General Requirements

A friend reported to me one day he had overheard someone remarking at the end of a lecture of mine that I possess "magnetic eyes." My eyes are, of course, quite ordinary, but the statement was significant, as similar remarks are commonly uttered concerning the hypnotists, on the assumption, I suppose, that it takes a special power to overcome the will of the subject and to put him into a trance. Nothing is further from the truth. Neither a special "power" is required to hypnotize, nor a peculiar "weakness" to be hypnotized. Scientific experiment and experience completely disprove this and similar popular notions as to the qualifications of persons involved in suggestion.

What science does find in this connection, is almost the very opposite of popular expectation. It is the subject's mental vigor rather than his weakness which favors the chances for success in hypnotic practice. I fully concur, in this regard, with C. L. Hull who says: "The popular belief that suggestibility is a mark of stupidity or lack of intelligence appears to be wholly an error so far as direct or prestige suggestion is concerned. Considerable experimental evidence indicates that, if anything, there is a slight positive relationship between suggestibility and intelligence."[1]   J. Milne Bramwell, too, says that he "found the stupid and unimaginative more difficult to influence than those possessing fair intelligence."[2]

It seems that direct suggestion requires an ability on the part of the subject to grasp the meaning of the hypnotist's instructions, and anything preventing such response makes practice so much more difficult. Insane people, as a rule, do not yield to suggestion as easily as do normal people, either because they shut themselves within their inner world, or because their minds are dim and incoherent, or else because their mental processes are too fast or too shifty to follow the steady process of verbal suggestion. Feeble-minded individuals, adults and children, are also exceedingly resistant to hypnosis.

Children of normal and superior intelligence are, on the whole, excellent subjects. Unless they are very young, boys and girls are somewhat more susceptible to suggestion than adults. Liébeault has practically demonstrated this fact by inducing hypnosis in every one of 88 children, ranging in age from 7 to 14, whereas other cases averaged success only in 9 cases out of 10. Though figures vary among later investigators, the rule is not seriously disputed.

Theoretically, it is true that "practically all normal persons can by hypnotized" and that "practically all

---

[1] *Hypnosis and Suggestibility,* 102.
[2] *Hypnotism,* 3rd ed., 63.

normal persons can learn to hypnotize."[3]   Even blind
and deaf people can be put into a trance, by a slight
modification of ordinary procedure.   Actually, however, no practician ever attains one hundred percent
success.   Failures are not due solely to deficiencies and
peculiarities of the subjects, nor to the hypnotist's
insufficient knowledge of, and experience in, handling
his cases skilfully and safely.   The situation itself may
arouse or create psychological forces that will prevent
the practician from establishing the necessary psychological relationship and, consequently, from succeeding
in putting across his suggestions, as the subject's habits
and memories can never be fully known or his reactions
and behavior fully predictable.   Nevertheless, proper
caution and technique will greatly help eliminate most
difficulties.

Since every one is, under ordinary circumstances,
suggestible, and since every one can also suggest, hypnosis, properly so called, is invariably a question of
proper relationship between at least two individuals.
This relationship is that of prestige-and-faith; that is to
say, the practician must possess sufficient confidence in
himself so as to carry and maintain prestige in the eyes
of his subjects, while the latter must have a sufficiently
firm faith in his ability to influence or cure them.   One's
success in practising hypnosis depends, therefore, on this
simple rule: *to establish and maintain the relationship
of prestige-and-faith.*   The ability to do so is useful in
all walks of life, especially in political and religious
leadership, in education and medical practice.   But it is
more than useful, it is indispensable in hypnotic prac-

---

[3] W. R. Wells, "Hypnosis in the Service of the Instructor," *Psychological Review*, 1924.

tice. If not mountains, faith moves men, women and children, in their mental as well as physical activities.

However, the relationship of prestige-and-faith cannot always be ordered into existence. Every so often the practician meets a person whose skepticism cannot be easily shaken by verbal persuasion or argument. What shall he do? Experience has taught me that a determined effort on the part of the subject to resist suggestion practically assures its failure. Consequently, I came to the conclusion never again to yield to the request or challenge of a skeptic to try him out, not until a change of mind has taken place. There are, certainly, ways to allay and overcome doubts. Where a direct approach is not sure, an indirect one may be of assistance. Or psychological preparation may be indicated. In this connection, W. F. Lovatt offers us an excellent, though not entirely new, method of handling a "doubting Thomas." Witness the following experience of his :[4]

"One of the spectators declared that no one would ever be able to have any influence over him, etc. . . . I said nothing to him for the time being, but after he had seen two other subjects quickly put to sleep, I suddenly turned to him and gave him a command to close his eyes. He did so at once. 'Now you can't open them', I suggested firmly. He couldn't in spite of trying hard. That same evening about an hour later he was no longer sceptical about suggestion and offered himself as a subject. In about three minutes he was deeply asleep and very suggestible. Today he is a very good and willing subject."

---

[4] *Hypnosis and Suggestion*, 21.

Some people are difficult to hypnotize as a result of their previous contacts with the practician. Among them are relatives, friends and even close acquaintances. It is an old truth that such persons, being on familiar terms with him, naturally feel "at home" in his company, which is a very pleasant thing in personal contacts, but in matters of suggestion it acts unfavorably. To them he is merely "Doc," Jim, dad, as the case may be: he is a man one can argue or disagree with. Before these individuals of the practician's own circle become fitting subjects, a certain psychological distance must be created. They should discover that the hypnotist is really a professional man, a scientist. They should be repeatedly placed among spectators (with the instruction to make no confidential statements) and thus be exposed to the contagion of prestige. They should be allowed to witness several trances.

The role of prestige-and-faith relationship is so great in hypnosis that no practician can afford to disregard the "atmosphere" in which he works and conducts his experiments or treatments. Every detail matters, and the subjects are much more sensitive to them than is generally believed. The place where the hypnotist receives his subjects must be carefully selected. Freud related in one of his books[5] that Bernheim, one of the most remarkable scientific hypnotists of all times, "frankly admitted to me that his great therapeutic successes by means of suggestion were only achieved in his hospital practice and not with his private patients." The reason for this fact is now obvious: the results of treatment depend on the subject's frame of mind. Any-

---

[5] *Autobiography*, 29.

thing that detracts from his faith, decreases the power
of suggestion over his mind and body. Consequently,
the hypnotist's home will not do as a place of practice,
nor surely the home of his subject, as neither is conducive to success, being too familiar, or ordinary, or
cozy. Suggestion is incomparably more effective in the
cold environment of an office. It should be preferably
impressive and stern in appearance, something that
makes people stay silent or talk in whispering tones. A
polite and business-like secretary will enhance the
effect. All apparatus should be prepared and arranged
in advance, to eliminate loss of time, fuss, muffled
swearing. The practician must leave in his subject's
mind the impression that he is certain of every motion
and step. The voice, too, must convey the importance,
exactitude, and calmness of his actions. The organization of his speech and the intonation of his words are
also not without significance.

These simple rules, though by no means compulsory
in every case, are so elementary that they are being
applied wherever suggestion is of value. Life imposes
them, in fact, upon virtually all professional men, in
their relations to clients. Any good physician, for
instance, knows that the atmosphere of his office
accounts for half of his success among patients, not
only from the monetary but also from the curative point
of view. And if he estimates soundly the role of these
seemingly irrelevant factors, he will not hesitate to pay
a high rent, to furnish his reception-room cleanly and
impressively, and even to purchase an automobile whose
make tends to magnify his prestige. That environment,
if properly selected, facilitates suggestion should be
best understood, of all people, by the hypnotist.

There is usually no serious reason for objecting to the presence of the subject's friends during a sitting. Quite the contrary, they often help to keep the patient's mind at ease. There are, in fact, persons (quite numerous, too) who feel a vague but strong apprehension that something might happen to them in the state of hypnotic "sleep." They commonly ask permission to bring a friend along, which request should be granted without hesitation. It happens occasionally that such visitors fall into a trance themselves, with no previous intention to be so influenced. This happens so frequently, in fact, that one concludes that the spectacle of hypnosis acts contagiously. For this reason, group sittings are generally quite successful, and the number of subjects, all hypnotized at once, is small handicap. These group sittings, however, should never be transformed into public demonstrations, unless there exists a special scientific purpose therefor.

B. Process of Hypnotizing

Once you have made up your mind to hypnotize a subject, be sure that there exists between you the relationship of prestige-and-faith. Furthermore, ascertain yourself that the subject is in good health. If you are not a physician, make him undergo a preliminary medical examination. Finally, take a written consent of your subject that he is willing to be hypnotized. This latter precaution is necessary mainly for your own protection.

When you, or still better your assistant or secretary, are through with these preliminaries, everything is ready for hypnotizing. How will you go about it?

Let it be understood that there exist countless techniques, all of which are equally good so long as they give confidence to the practician and faith to the subject. The only purpose of any method of hypnotizing is to concentrate the subject's attention and thus to eliminate most of the disturbing influences while leaving but a single channel of suggestion, which is usually the voice of the hypnotist and the ear of the subject.

I shall describe, to begin with, a simple method which I found quite practicable and convenient, and then, if the reader wishes to modify it or to select some other technique successfully used by some authority in the field, he is welcome and free to do so. He knows best the circumstances under which he intends to work.

The subject must be put at ease, not only mentally but also physically. He may be placed in a comfortable arm chair, where his head rests in such a manner as to make breathing and swallowing effortless. People are in the habit of swallowing saliva at the beginning of a sitting, and their normal progress toward the hypnotic state is handicapped if their heads are in a strained position. Besides, the neck muscles relax as soon as the subject enters the state; and unless his head rests comfortably, its falling on the chest or on the back of the chair may arouse him.

No strong sensation should disturb the subject. In other words, light should not shine directly into his eyes and all superfluous noises should be eliminated, if possible, while the temperature of the room should be pleasantly warm.

Let me say a few words concerning the apparatus. Place a small ball, the size of an ordinary button, reflecting light toward the subject, so as to raise his eyes slightly upward to concentrate his attention. The ball so placed is conducive to fatiguing one's eyes which, incidentally, occupy approximately the same position as in ordinary sleep.

So-called "passes,"[6] extensively used in the nineteenth century, are quite superfluous, unless the subject had been made to believe in their power. Nor is there any need to hold a hand on the subject's forehead, hand or knee; in general, no bodily contact is required. One's voice is a sufficient channel of communication for suggestion. If, however, you want to be sure of the normal heart-beat of your patient, have your fingers on his pulse.

Pre-hypnotic suggestions should begin soon or even immediately after the subject is placed in the chair. You may be saying, for example, something of this sort: "Look steadily at the ball in front of you. Look steadily and do not wink. After a while your eyes will become weary and shut by themselves. Do not try to close them deliberately, nor make any efforts to keep them open. Forget about everything except that you must look at the ball. I shall be watching you closely, to help you enter the state of hypnosis. When you are ready, I shall say 'Keep your eyes closed'. As you enter the state, your entire organism will cooperate with the suggestions I am going to give you. You will find it a calm, pleasant state, during which you enjoy thorough relaxation. But you will be aware of everything I say and of everything you do. Now relax, feel well. Let your breathing be light; let your heart beat evenly, just as in the state of normal sleep. Your eyes

---

[6] Symmetric movements of the hypnotist's arms, which were thought to be connected with "magnetic waves."

are getting tired, but they will be relieved now that a pleasant drowsiness envelops you."

Unless you give these or similar pre-hypnotic suggestions, the subject might develop uneasiness and manifest unpleasant sensations from which the practician ought to protect him. There is no reason why the hypnotic state should not be effective as well as pleasant. I remember my first attempt at hypnotizing, when I knew very little of what to expect. The subject, a young man of twenty, entered the state surprisingly easily but immediately afterward began to groan and to move about. Naturally, I became somewhat frightened and decided immediately to awake him. But for a minute or so, neither could he get out of the trance nor could I arouse him. Nothing more serious happened, of course; nevertheless, I promised myself to take, henceforth, every precaution against similar accidents.

Most hypnotists seem to encourage and actually to suggest amnesia subsequent to the sitting. Occasionally there may be, I grant, a need for doing so. But in most cases it is quite superfluous, in my opinion, to give the subject a pre-hypnotic suggestion to forget whatever will have happened during the trance. With Schilder and Kauders, I contend that "we do not consider it an advantage to have the patient kept in ignorance of what is happening to him."[7] I object to the traditional tendency on purely practical grounds. I do not know of any advantage in producing amnesia in *every* case. But I do know from experience that a suggestion contrary to the customary practice, namely, a suggestion *to remember* everything that happens

---

[7] *Hypnosis,* 88.

during the state, actually increases the practician's chances for success and shortens the pre-hypnotic period. I have often observed a marked decrease of tension immediately after such a suggestion. It has an additional importance in that it counteracts the tendency among persons able to recall their experiences during the state to deny subsequently that they had been hypnotized at all.

The above description of hypnotic technique is merely an example. Most other methods successfully used in the past do not differ greatly from the one just described. But they contain features which may be occasionally used with advantage. It is desirable to be acquainted with their distinct characteristics; but we shall not go here into a discussion of minute details.

1. When the method of "fascination" is used (the earlier experimenters, including Braid and Bernheim), the practician and his subject gaze steadily into each other's eyes, until the latter enters the trance. The hypnotist, naturally, does not succumb first, because he has all the advantages of position, prestige and experience. The eyes here play the role of the ball; but any object of concentration can be used in their place, such as button, pencil, tip of one's own nose, or some specially constructed apparatus. J. Luys used revolving mirrors, with increased visual stimulation at regular intervals.

2. Vision is not the only sense that can be employed for concentration of attention. Touch and even smell and taste provide the means for it, but only hearing has been used more or less extensively for the purpose (Van Eeden, among others). The subject is approached and treated, on the whole, in the manner described

above, but instead of concentrating his eyes on some visible object, he is asked to attend closely, for instance, to the ticking of a watch; or to count numbers aloud, beginning with one, two, three, until he enters the trance; even mere listening to the voice of the practician may suffice. An interesting case is reported by Dorcus and Shaffer:[8] "One subject whom the writer had attempted to hypnotize but who could not be thrown into the trance state by visual fixation and the usual verbal stimuli, however, when left alone for about five minutes with the instruction to listen very carefully to the ticking of a watch placed behind him was found in a fairly deep hypnotic state upon my return to the room."

3. Some hypnotists (Liébeault, Charcot, Bernheim, Forel and, especially, Bechterew) advocated to break the period of strained attention with a sudden change in experience, by sending a strong beam of light into the subject's eyes, by sounding a gong, or by a sharp command, "Sleep!" The advantages of this method have not been clearly determined. It seems to precipitate the state at an earlier stage than with the usual procedure, but it entails risk of failure, if the moment is wrongly chosen. This technique is recommended, however, in cases when the subject appears to vacillate on the verge of the trance and closes his eyes only to open them again and again. The point is to watch the subject closely and to push him, as it were, into the state. The method requires considerable experience, and beginners should be discouraged from resorting to it. Even specialists should use it with discrimination.

---

[8] *Textbook of Abnormal Psychology,* 177.

4. If the subject has been repeatedly hypnotized, the trance can be induced very easily, sometimes merely by reminding him of a previous similar experience. In fact, the facility with which it can be induced grows with every sitting up to a certain point. Subjects have been known to be hypnotized by telephone or letter (Liégeois). Victrola records have been used to the same effect.[9] And it is not inconceivable that hypnosis will be effected by a radio broadcast. I hope to see the experiment attempted; I do not mind even to try my own hand, should an opportunity present itself.

5. In some cases requiring medical treatment, drugs may be of valuable assistance, as facilitating the process of hypnotizing. Alcohol and also chloroform, chloral hydrate (5 grains), paraldehyde (20 mms.), veronal (½ grain), and cannabis indica (1½ grain) have been used with considerable success (Esdaile, Schrenck-Notzing, Herrero, Bernheim, Jastrow, and others). All systematic use of chemicals should be discouraged, however, and the physician-hypnotist should resort to their application only in exceptional cases. In experiments, too, the practician should avoid drugs, unless the procedure be specially devised, following a careful estimate of the narcotic effect. Drugs will raise the percentage of successful hypnotization, to be sure; but, on the other hand, the significance of the results may be thereby greatly obscured. It then becomes somewhat difficult to determine precisely what role was played by the drug and what by the suggestion, and also to what extent did the narcotics interfere with the hypnotic regulation of bodily processes.

---

[9] G. H. Estabrooks, "A Standardized Hypnotic Technique Dictated to a Victrola Record," *The American Journal of Psychology*, 1930.

C.   In the State

A little experience will enable the practician to recognize easily the oncoming hypnotic state. The typical sign is the closing of the eyes, sudden or gradual. Often it is accompanied by a peculiar quivering of the lids, that usually ceases in a minute or two. Or the eyes may be closed tightly. This symptom cannot be regarded, however, as certain, sufficient, or even necessary. It is most common, because the hypnotist suggests it almost invariably from the beginning. But it is quite possible for the subject to enter the trance with his eyes half-shut or fully open, and it is easy also to make him open his eyes during the state, without disturbing him in the least. Among other symptoms that are observable, we find the upward movement of the eyeballs, the deepening of the breathing, general facial relaxation, etc.

The beginner should not be impatient. He must be prepared to wait ten, fifteen, or more minutes before his subject enters the trance. Nor should he relieve the feeling of uncertainty by challenging his subject, "You cannot open your eyes. No matter how hard you try it, you cannot." Especially bad is to add contradiction to mistake, by persisting, "Well, try it!" As a matter of fact, if the assertion is made before the subject is really in the state, he usually does open his eyes. As a result, the practician's prestige may be lowered, and the chances for success seriously diminished. I am, therefore, more than in agreement with Professor McDougall who remarked, "Challenge to movement in this early stage is a doubtful policy. If the suggestion fails, the failure is prejudicial, though not necessarily fatal, to the success of further suggestion."[10]

As soon as the state is reached, it is time to begin with systematic suggestions. Their nature and content, of course, depend on the case and the practician's intentions. But I should like to give the following advice, in regard to form. Unless the situation calls specifically for the opposite procedure, suggestions should not be given as mere orders, for no matter how deep the trance may be, a human being resents being commanded and manifests resistance, if in disagreement. In fact, it should never be forgotten that one addresses, even in hypnosis, a being behaving according to certain psychological laws. Rather than order the subject about, the practician should offer him firm and wise leadership. Suggestions, strong, definite and clear, should be given in as natural a way as possible. Through a careful and realistic approach, with the subject's own views as the starting point, he can be convinced of many a thing which he might reject as impossible or ridiculous if approached bluntly, without due preparation and transition. Nothing is cruder in suggestion than to command, for instance: "You must imagine you are travelling in a train. You must. You must!" I have seen persons under hypnosis, who smiled at such commands in a way indicating beyond doubt that their ability to criticize, and differ with, the practician is not totally absent in the trance. How much finer it is to convey the same idea in a casual, conversational manner, such as: "I like to travel in trains. I get the feeling of doing something adventurous, and look forward to seeing new

---

[10] *Outline of Abnormal Psychology,* 86.

faces, new places. When I am alone in the compart-
ment, it seldom occurs to me to read a newspaper or
magazine. Like a little boy, I eagerly look out of the
window and find so many interesting things to observe,
to admire." Before you complete the monologue and
come to the intended suggestion, the subject already
shares your imaginary experiences. The picture is in
his mind, realistic and personal, before you have had a
chance to express it fully.

If the purpose of the sitting is to stimulate an emotional attitude, as when the patient is to be cured of an
objectionable habit, such as nail-biting or smoking, when
he must be taught to feel disgust or aversion to the
object of his addiction, the emotion should be aroused
by some visual image or by some imaginary yet realistic experience, rather than be suggested merely in
words. A hypnotist will do wisely to memorize a
number of stories that can serve the purpose. "When I
suggest anger," write Schilder and Kauders,[11] "I never
suggest this feeling alone, but must always suggest a
content of reproduction or of conception together with
the idea. In fact, in general, much better results will
be obtained in suggestions of this type by emphasizing
the content and not the feeling of the emotion as such. . .
This attitude simultaneously furnishes us with the
general formulation that every conception, every perception, every idea, has its appropriate vasovegetative
consequences. . . If I desire an acceleration of my
heart-beat, I can attain it by visualizing a terrifying
conception." To a scientist well versed in the functional mechanism of human psychology, such a pro-

---

[11] *Hypnosis,* 16.

cedure is not a novel device, but an old and basic rule of suggestion.

While suggestions are being given, the hypnotist should watch his subject closely. If he happens to feel uneasy or desires to make some important statement, he is not always able to manifest his wishes sufficiently plainly to attract the hypnotist's attention. Often his muscles are paralyzed for every practical purpose except to follow instructions given him. Nevertheless, motor impulses may succeed, not unlike in ordinary sleep, in breaking through the ties of inhibition and in producing a groan, a movement of the head, or result in some other slight indication. Five years ago I conducted a group experiment in education under oneirosis (a species of light hypnosis[12]). Soon after I began to lecture, I noticed that one of my subjects, a girl already in the trance, moved her little finger again and again. The movements were merely incipient, but sufficiently obvious to make me realize that the girl wanted to express something or to communicate with me, but was unable to break the ties of muscular inhibition. I immediately interrupted the experiment, awoke her, and was told she was trying hard to inform me that I was talking too fast.

Some experiments and treatments, as in the above instance, do not require the subject to produce any movements at all. He remains sitting in the chair, seemingly passive, with his eyes shut. Other cases call for various motions. Muscular inhibition, it seems, can be created or abolished practically at will; the practician's suggestion suffices to paralyze or to stimulate a muscle.

---

[12] See Chapter 8.

Occasionally it is desirable to make the subject speak. Neurotic patients, for instance, may suffer from repressions or complexes rooted in their childhood experiences. In order to bring back these distant memories and thus to relieve an ailment or to give a clue to it, the subject is asked relevant questions and is urged to tell whatever episodes he can recall. In the terminology of Breuer and the phychoanalysts, this procedure is known as "catharsis", can be used with or without hypnosis, and is supposed to bring a "psychic trauma" back to consciousness and let it work itself off. I disagree with Freud's interpretation of the phenomenon, but the method helps, indeed, to remove old inhibitions. Whereas the subject in the trance is unable to say a word on his own initiative and appears to be, as it were, totally mute, his faculty of speech is restored almost instantaneously, as soon as the practician says, "I wish to ask you several questions. Tell me, please . . ." For several seconds the subject may have visible and audible difficulties, but soon he overcomes all the handicaps, and speech flows henceforth almost as freely as in natural conditions, though perhaps in a somewhat slower tempo; and even these remaining peculiarities can be removed by additional suggestion. If necessary, the subject can also be made to write, to walk, and to perform other actions, simple or complex, depending on what suggestion is given. And throughout the performance, he remains in the trance, keenly susceptible to the hypnotist's directions, till he is finally aroused from the state.

D.   Ending the State

The hypnotic state can be prolonged almost in-definitely, without fear that the subject might incur harmful effects. The practician will find, however, that all he needs, in most instances, to imprint his sugges-tions upon the subject's mind and through it upon the subject's autonomic nervous system, is five minutes. He may be willing to spend an hour or two keeping the subject in the trance. He may transfer the power of suggestion (or "rapport," as it is called technically). Or he may even leave the subject alone in the state, until he comes back. But sooner or later the trance must be broken, and the normal waking state restored.

Occasionally it happens—when the practician loses his confidence, for example—that it is difficult to arouse the subject from the trance. The situation may be quite disconcerting and, if the sitting is performed in public, highly embarrassing. Nevertheless, there is no ground for worry. The trance normally passes into natural sleep, out of which the subject emerges spon-taneously or can be easily awakened after a while. The few cases on record of an exceptionally prolonged sleep (lasting for hours or even days) represent rare excep-tions and have really nothing to do with hypnosis: they must be considered as due to hysteria.

How does one end the trance? Ordinarily it is sufficient to say, "Open your eyes," and to repeat the phrase emphatically if necessary, and the subject is back in his normal state, ready to report his experiences or to go home. He may feel somewhat bewildered or drowsy. In fact, it has been pointed out that "it is quite general for subjects to show a slightly dazed appearance, upon first being roused from deep trance. As a matter of fact, subjects do not really wake instantly, as is sometimes thought by superficial observers of a trance demonstration. On the contrary, it is evident that the influence of the trance persists for some little time after they have responded to the command to wake by opening their eyes. This is probably why subjects can be thrown into a trance very much more readily a minute or so after waking from one than a day or two after."[18]

Even this daze or somnolence can be easily avoided, however, if a proper suggestion is given just a few seconds before waking the subject. In fact, such a suggestion should be administered as a part of regular hypnotic procedure. The practician may say, for instance: "This sitting is concluded and presently I shall wake you up. But before I do so, I want to impress upon your mind that you are going to feel well and wide awake for the rest of the day. You will be able to examine the hypnotic experience in retrospection and to appreciate the results. Now open your eyes. Open your eyes!" And on the complete awakening of the subject, when he regains his orientation, you will give him necessary instructions, according to the case, and then dismiss him by saying: "Thank you for your cooperation. You may go now. And don't forget, I rely upon your feeling well."

Early in my research, I used to indulge in conversation with my subjects aroused from the state. But experience taught me that it is not advisable to be simple and frank with the subjects and, especially, to discuss

---

[18] Hull, *Hypnosis and Suggestibility*, 33.

hypnosis. Good relations with them, if necessary, must be sacrificed to maintain right relations. Prestige-and-faith is an attitude that should be preserved, and familiarity is one of its most deadly enemies. The subject will discuss his experiences anyway, but let him do so with outsiders. If he is curious to comprehend the phenomena of suggestion and hypnosis, he will find enough information in books like this. I cannot explain them any clearer by word of mouth.

E. Post-Hypnotic Suggestion

The expression, "post-hypnotic suggestion," is somewhat misleading. Really it refers not to suggestions given after the trance, but to those offered during it to be executed subsequently. Bernheim described the phenomenon in his *Suggestive Therapeutics* as "inducing in somnambulists by means of suggestion, acts, illusions of the senses, and hallucinations which shall not be manifested during the sleeping condition, but upon waking."

The first scientists who studied the phenomenon were Liébeault, Richet, Bernheim, and Delboeuf. Their principle interest was amnesia. They discovered that one of the most common results of deep hypnosis is a complete inability on the part of the patient to recall anything that transpired during the sitting. Soon they found also that an appropriate suggestion during the trance will produce the same effect, even if the state was not very deep.

Amnesia was originally regarded as essential to all post-hypnotic suggestion. Even today it is usually asserted that "post-hypnotic commands are as a rule

better executed if amnesia is present."[14]   This is doubtless true whenever the subject is asked to do something
unusual or absurd.   For were he to remember instructions distinctly, not only would his common sense resent
the suggestion as clearly strange or foolish, but even
the prestige of the practician might be damaged by
doubts and resistance. Suppose the subject is instructed,
on hearing the word "sunset," to stand on a chair and
to sing some popular song in a loud voice.   As the
order is being executed, he may regard it as a joke, but
still he will not deny that his conduct, at the moment,
was somewhat ridiculous.   And he will perhaps wonder
what might be the connection between scientific research
and such meaningless experiments.

There is no need, however, to be engaged in trifling
experiments.   Hypnosis is, after all, a natural phenomenon rather than entertainment.   There certainly are
many serious and fruitful fields for post-hypnotic suggestion.   The phenomenon can be studied without
resorting to the unusual and the absurd. In most studies
along scientific lines, amnesia becomes superfluous, as
the subject, realizing the importance of the given suggestion, is willing to cooperate with the practician, consciously and gladly.   The practice of autosuggestion, as
popularized by E. Coué and his New Nancy School,
has sufficiently substantiated the contention that, whenever one concentrates his mind upon something he
eagerly desires to modify in his behavior or in the
functions of his organism, a conscious realization of
intentions is no handicap at all.

Amnesia, as an automatic result of deep trance or as

---

[14] Schilder and Kauders, *Hypnosis*, 59.

an intentional inhibition of memory, remains of considerable interest to us.   But we also begin to discover that post-hypnotic suggestion has a positive value, that numerous things can be accomplished through it in medicine, psychology and education.   We find here a definite proof that human behavior depends largely on the autonomic nervous system, in its effects upon the mind and body, and also that physiological processes, no less than conscious activities, are constantly being conditioned by suggestion.

Clinical literature is full of examples of such conditioning.   The subject is asked, for instance, to wake up on the following morning precisely at three o'clock, to take a book and read for fifteen minutes.   In order to make the experiment conclusive and convincing, he may be instructed to forget about the order, but to execute it as it were spontaneously.   True enough, the subject wakes up at the indicated time and does everything exactly as instructed.   Afterwards, if asked why he did it, he will, in all probability, retort that there was really nothing extraordinary about his actions. He simply woke up and, feeling that he would not be able to go back to sleep immediately, decided to take a book and to read for a while.   The human power of rationalization is truly amazing, and men tend to explain away anything that does not suit their purposes or evades their comprehension.

One of the most important consequences of post-hypnotic suggestion is the increased susceptibility of the subject to the practician's directions.   Whenever the subject must be hypnotized repeatedly, it is always desirable to shorten the pre-hypnotic period.   The procedure becomes easier with every sitting.   But it will be truly of negligible duration, if the practician tells his subject, just before arousing him from the preceding trance, to enter the state practically instantaneously at the next sitting. As a result, it sometimes suffices to snap the fingers, and the subject is immediately in a trance.

Post-hypnotic suggestion can render the subject completely anaesthetic to certain experiences in the waking state. H. Lundholm, for instance, demonstrated[15] that the subject can be trained to be fully deaf to a click. I had several interesting cases of this sort. I recall a young man, neurotic, who had been in a state of utter misery for years, as the experience of seeing or hearing people spit produced violent disgust and nausea in him. He tried to pay no attention to what happened on the street. But the more he tried, the more hopeless were the efforts: the walking on the streets became the agony of fearful expectation. Then he came to me. In several sittings he was trained to disregard the thing, even if it happened right in front of him.

One of the richest fields for post-hypnotic suggestion is, evidently, that of objectionable habits. In fact, no adequate treatment of these ailments is possible apart from such suggestion, whether it be alcoholism, smoking, drug addiction, nail-biting, or what not. But almost invariably the practician is confronted with one great difficulty: post-hypnotic suggestion does not seem to last indefinitely. It follows a curve of obliviscence; that is to say, the strength of suggestion clearly diminishes, at first rapidly and then slowly. Whereas time is

[15] "An Experimental Study of Functional Anesthesias as Induced by Suggestion in Hypnosis," *Journal of Abnormal and Social Psychology,* 1928.

comparatively of small significance when a post-hypnotic suggestion refers to a definite action at a specified time (be it months or even years after the direction was given), any general instruction is subject to an entirely different rule, especially when the objectionable habit is based on a strong urge or temptation. My observation is that, in such cases, suggestion is seldom reliable beyond three weeks, though the period somewhat differs in each instance.

What can be done, then, to attain a greater degree of reliability in treating objectionable habits? It is possible, of course, to renew the suggestion every once in a while, by hypnotizing the subject at regular intervals; yet it is often inconvenient to the subject as well as to the practician to repeat sittings beyond three or four times. Besides, as pointed out by O. H. Mowrer,[16] there is some danger that the efficacy of post-hypnotic suggestion will be reduced by repeated sittings.

Fortunately, the excessive repetition of sittings can be avoided through a simple device of auto-suggestion. Suppose a patient is treated by hypnosis for the habit of excessive smoking. While in the state, he is given a cigarette to smoke and conditioned, say, to the emotion of disgust. In order to re-arouse this feeling at regular intervals, without subjecting him to further treatments, he is given, on being awakened from the trance, a note-book on the cover of which a label is attached, with the following words conspicuously printed:

---

[16] "A Note on the Effect of Repeated Hypnotic Stimulation," *Journal of Abnormal and Social Psychology,* 1932.

MY DAILY REPORT
ON THE TREATMENT OF
THE HABIT OF SMOKING

As the patient receives this note-book, he is instructed as follows: "It is very important that you make a daily report on the progress of your cure, even it it be 'No change'. This note-book will help you a good deal, by reminding you of the suggestion you have now received from me. Every time you take the book to write down your report, read carefully the title. On this date next month, come to see me again." As all suggestion is rooted in the functions of the autonomic nervous system, such use of auto-suggestion can often be properly and advantageously combined with hypnosis.

CHAPTER VII

Dangers of Hypnosis

Since James Braid found that hypnosis is unbelievably harmless for a power so remarkable and great, his contention has remained virtually unshaken. Despite the low opinion of hypnotism held by the public, manifested both in its idle curiosity and its evil-humored gossip, there have been reported amazingly few instances of ill-effects. Moreover, of the few that have actually occurred, most, if not all, should be attributed to accident or coincidence. In a recent study of this problem, M. H. Erickson states,[1] "The literature offers little credible information concerning possible detrimental effects of experimental hypnosis, although replete with dogmatic and opinionated denunciations founded on outworn and untenable concepts of the phenomenon. The author's own experience, based upon several thousand trances on approximately three hundred individual subjects, some of whom were hypnotized at least five hundred times each over a period of four to six years, reveals no evidence of such harmful effects. The clinical finding is further substantiated by the well-known difficulties encountered in the deliberate therapeutic attempts to occasion desired changes in the personality. Accordingly, marked changes from experimental hypnosis appear questionable."

[1] "Possible Detrimental Effects of Experimental Hypnosis," *The Journal of Abnormal and Social Psychology,* 1932.

Emotional agitation which naturally accompanies the expectation of being hypnotized for the first time should alone lead, as it seems, to unpleasant consequences and accidents. Fortunately for all concerned, this danger finds its antidote in the fact that hypnotic suggestion, properly controlled, is soothing. As J. B. Dynes says,[2] "the hypnotic trance acts as a quieting influence." I have found, in my experience, nothing to contradict this observation.

No more truth is found in the contention, often heard in popular discussions, that hypnosis undermines the will of the subject and, when the sittings are regularly repeated, makes him hypersuggestible, a slave, as it were, to the commands of the practician. This contention is merely a vicious superstition of long standing, with no facts available to confirm it. A careful study of effects has substantiated, contrariwise, the enlightened opinion of scientists, that hypnosis has no known psychological ill-effects on the subjects. "Far from making them hypersuggestible," says Dr. Erickson, "it was found necessary to deal very gingerly with them to keep from losing their cooperation and it was often felt that they developed a compensatory negativism toward the hypnotist to offset any increased suggestibility."

The following case illustrates this psychological tendency. "Miss G., aged 19, an uneducated girl, had been frequently hypnotized, and was a good somnambule. She had had sixteen teeth extracted at Leeds during hypnotic anaesthesia. At a later date, having examined her mouth and found that a fragment of one of the stumps remained, I asked her to come to my house

---

[2] "An Experimental Study in Hypnotic Anaesthesia," *Journal of Abnormal and Social Psychology*, 1932.

to have it removed. She mentioned this to one of her neighbors, an old woman, who advised her to have no more teeth extracted, as this would cause her mouth to fall in. The following day she presented herself, and was at once hypnotized; she refused to open her mouth, or to permit me to extract the tooth. Emphatic suggestion continued for half an hour produced no result. This was the first occasion on which she had rejected a suggestion. I then awoke her, and asked why she refused to have the tooth extracted. She told me what her neighbor had said, and expressed her determination to have nothing more done. I explained the absurdity of this, and pointed out that, as she had only the fragment of one tooth remaining, its removal could not affect the appearance of her face. As she was still obstinate, I said: "Unless this fragment is removed you cannot have your artificial teeth fitted'. This argument was sufficient. She gave her consent in the waking state, was at once hypnotized, and operated on without pain."[8]

This surprising lack of harmful effects of scientific hypnosis has been observed and commented upon by such noted authorities as Liébeault, Wetterstrand, van Eeden, de Jong, Moll, Bramwell, Schilder and Kauders. A. Forel asserted that he has never come across a single instance of physical or mental harm caused by hypnosis. Bernheim recorded but on case (*Revue Médicale de l'Est,* for February, 1895), "in which death followed hypnosis induced by a medical man. The patient suffered from phlebitis, accompanied by severe pain; and to relieve this, Bernheim hypnotized him. He died two

---

[8] J. M. Bramwell, *Hypnotism,* 315-16.

hours afterwards, and post-mortem examination showed that death was due to embolism of the pulmonary artery. . . Bernheim has hypnotized over 10,000 hospital patients; sometimes this would be done for relief of pain associated with inevitably fatal maladies, and, therefore, the matter for surprise is that death has not more frequently occurred during, or shortly after, the induction of hypnosis."[4]

An interesting passage is found in one of Munthe's books,[5] who wrote: "Most of the accusations against hypnotism are greatly exaggerated. So far I know of no well authenticated proof of a criminal act committed by a subject under hypnotic suggestion. I have never seen a suggestion made under hypnosis carried out by the subject which he or she would refuse to carry out if made during normal waking state. I affirm that if a blackguard should suggest to a woman under profound hypnosis that she should surrender herself to him and she should carry out this suggestion, it would mean that she would as readily have done so had the suggestion been made to her in a normal condition of waking life. There is no such thing as blind obedience. The subject knows quite well what is going on the whole time and what he is willing or unwilling to do. Camille, Professor Liégeois' famous somnambulist in Nancy, who would remain impassive and indifferent when a pin was stuck full length through her arm or a piece of burning charcoal put in her hand, would blush scarlet when the Professor pretended to make a gesture as if to disarrange her clothes, and wake up instantaneously. This is only one of the many baffling contradictions

---

[4] Quoted from Bramwell, op. cit., 426.
[5] *The Story of San Michele*, 322.

familiar to students of hypnotic phenomena and most difficult for the outsiders to understand. The fact that the person cannot be hypnotized without his or her will, must not be overlooked by the alarmists. Of course all talk about an unwilling and unaware person being hypnotized at a distance is sheer nonsense."

Thus, the harmlessness of hypnosis is as firmly established as it could be. Nevertheless, no matter how small the danger of the trance may be, caution should not be forgotten, the more so that, in case the practician is accused by a subject or his relative—rightly or wrongly—of having done him some physical, moral or financial damage, public opinion is sure to be antagonistic to the practician.

Therefore, I recommend the following simple rules of caution:

1. Never to attempt the practice of hypnosis before one has made a thorough and minute study of the field;

2. Never to hypnotize unless one is a physician, psychologist or educator;

3. To avoid superfluous public demonstrations of the art of suggestion;

4. To practise hypnosis only as an essential part of scientific research;

5. To take invariably, before the first sitting, the written consent of the subject or of his parents, if he be a minor;

6. To make all appropriate pre-hypnotic, hypnotic and post-hypnotic suggestions protecting the subject's mental and physical health; and

7. To discontinue experiments with subjects who had manifested a physical indisposition during the trance.

The above measures of precaution, if faithfully followed, are quite sufficient to make hypnotic experimentation, study and practice as harmless as it can be. They also serve to safeguard the scholar and practician in his useful work from the tongue of ignorant, biassed and fanatical persons. To make it completely clear from what public accusations these rules protect the practician, let me quote a case from A. Moll, who made an extensive study of the legal aspects of hypnotism.

"A hypnotizer and professional healer, who used to give 'suggestion parties' at his house in Hanover, in 1905, was condemned for causing one of his subjects bodily injury through neglect. At these entertainments he had performed most unwarrantable experiments on a work-girl, suggesting among other things that a man would undress in front of her to bathe, then jump into the water and be drowned. As the girl was taken seriously ill after the experiments, the experimenter was charged and convicted."[6]

There are cases of another type, in which the hypnotist cannot be justly accused of levity or insufficient caution. "Every medical man who has had any considerable experience in the domain of hypnosis has probably come across laymen who endeavor to ascribe to hypnosis anything they find very peculiar, or for some reason or other unpleasant, or that they cannot quite understand. At times it is a case of seduction or a mysterious love affair, at others the provisions of a will or the exploitation of some business, that puzzles them."[7] Needless to say, accusations of this sort are, as a rule, wholly imaginary, and hint of mental disease,

---

[6] *Hypnosis,* 410.
[7] *Ibid.,* 413.

such as schizophrenia or hysteria.   A competent psychi-
atrist should be immediately consulted.

In view of these facts, I concur fully with Dr. Moll
in his opinion that public exhibitions of hypnosis "ought
to be prohibited on both moral and hygienic grounds.
It is perfectly true that at one time such public exhibitions served to draw the attention of scientists to hypnotism, but nowadays they are more calculated to repel
people from the scientific study of that question, since
they degrade hypnosis into an object of vulgar curiosity, instead of elevating it to one of research."[8]   The
only type of demonstration that should be permitted is
that of scientific nature and of educational purport.

Not only do I recommend practicians in hypnosis
to take every sort of precaution for the sake of their
patients and themselves; I also urge them to discourage
every sign of a frivolous attitude toward this interesting field among their acquaintances and students, and
to fight the abuse of hypnotic power by unscrupulous
persons pursuing satisfaction of their vanity or an
increase of income, rather than growth of knowledge
and understanding.   Not that hypnosis offers a rich
field for abuse.   As we have already seen, it is naturally
protected against charlatans and criminals, both in
regard to physical safety and moral corruption. Nevertheless, this protection is far from being sufficient.   On·
the whole, it is true, as most scientific hypnotists assume,
that the subject himself revolts against being forced to
commit immoral or anti-social acts.   But this is true
only under normal and ordinary conditions.   The possibility still remains that, in evil and skilful hands, sug-

---

[8] *Ibid.,* 440.

gestion can be used as a tool of considerable harmfulness.

The reason for the erroneous generalization drawn by many authorities on the subject lies in the inadequacy of their information. The evidence they have collected has almost invariably been insufficient, and in their own experiments they have commonly sinned against the simplest laws of suggestion. If a hypnotized subject is instructed in a crude fashion, such as "Go to this house and steal the necklace that lies in the top drawer of a dresser, second room to the right," he surely will not obey, unless, perhaps, he is a habitual thief. For some unknown reason, hypnotists commonly assume that the tone of sharp command is the most effective method of securing a blind obedience of the subject. In this they are not fully wrong. Firmness is recommended, no doubt, yet orders are obeyed only when the atmosphere of willing cooperation or that of animal fear has already been established. Surely, the emotion of fear is not the standard means of scientific suggestion. The remaining way of willing cooperation is much more desirable as well as effective.

It appears self-evident that whatever can be done in the normal waking state by means of ordinary suggestion, can also be done in the hypnotic state. Suppose you are told—in the normal waking state, mind you— by a person you have no grounds to distrust and may even respect: "Bring my pocket-book, please, do you mind? It is in the side pocket of my coat, in the next room." Might you not go there and bring the pocket-book, even if it does not belong to the person asking you to do so (which fact is, of course, unknown to you)? Can't you thus be made an innocent accomplice of a theft? The history of criminal law is replete with acts of larceny, burglary and fraud, in which people are mixed up as innocent victims of suggestion. If suggestion has sufficient power to lead men to unintentional crimes apart from hypnosis, don't say it cannot be done in a trance.

I contend that the subject can even be made to commit murder under hypnosis—or, rather, an unintentional homicide, if you please—if the suggestion in question is given in a manner misleading the senses or concealing the final result. To make the argument more conclusive, suppose you are challenged (in the normal waking state, again) to play a practical joke on a friend of yours, by putting some sleeping powder (or laxative) into his coffee. You may be tempted to do so, if you are in a proper frame of mind. And in all probability you will not investigate to discover whether the powder you had been handed is actually a harmless somniferous drug. It might be a poison! Now, if there is a chance of being made an unconscious partner to a murder plot in ordinary circumstances, there is obviously a greater probability of being so fooled under hypnosis. And perhaps to be made to forget the act!

We are justified in concluding, therefore, that the resistance of a person in a trance to improper suggestions is strong only as long as he is asked *directly* to violate his economic, moral, religious, or aesthetic convictions and interests. But he can be influenced to go against these convictions and interests, if his senses are deceived, if he acts under false assumptions, or if he is unaware of the implications of his conduct. His mistake—that is what it amounts to—may be disastrous, though natural, under special circumstances. The plain truth of the whole problem is, in the words of C. Baudouin,[9] that any subject will follow a suggestion if he "imagines it to be possible."   But he will resist or disobey a suggestion to do anything that he would not do ordinarily, if the act is presented as such.

It is fallacious, I think, to assume that there are fields of knowledge which are perfectly safe.   None is. Every science and profession is good only in so far as it is used for good purposes.   Human genius has been known to turn the best things into sources of evil and destruction.   Explosives, airplanes and submarines can be used to promote civilization or to take human lives in war.   Industrial inventions can be operated to increase prosperity or to deprive people of the means of livelihood.   Drugs can be and have been used not to restore health but to impair it.   Laws can be and are being made to dispense injustice rather than justice. Political power can oppress or liberate.   These facts give us no reason, however, to repress research and experimentation.   The benefits of science, in all its forms and branches, outweigh immensely its occasional detriments.   This surely holds true of hypnotism, too. Hypnotism is one of the sciences, with everything that this word implies.   It is harmless in itself, as has been fully demonstrated in the above pages, but in certain cases of negligence or evil intention it becomes, like all good things, a source of harm.

---

[9] *Suggestion and Autosuggestion,* 1922. p. 242.

CHAPTER VIII

Oneirosis, A Form of Hypnosis

Hypnosis does not present a uniform phenomenon. Being a creature of suggestion, it varies with the practician, subject and circumstances. One of the most obvious distinctions is that of intensity. It is quite important, not because it helps in description, but because the state admits of an easy control in regard to its depth. Classifications of the trance according to its intensity are old. The most familiar one is that of A. Forel who, following somewhat complex classifications of A. Liébeault and H. Bernheim, discriminated among the incipient trance (also called somnolence or, in B. Sidis's terminology, the hypnoidal state), light hypnosis (hypotaxis), and deep hypnosis (somnambulism).

It was customary to believe that opportunities of hypnotic experimentation multiply and improve with the greater depth of the trance. Consequently, the practicians were seldom satisfied with mere somnolence, but sought to produce somnambulism in every case. As far as popular demonstrations are concerned, this prejudicial attitude still persists, for an obvious reason: for commercial purposes, nothing but the spectacular will do. What is, indeed, more amusing and startling to an excitement-seeking gathering than to watch a subject making a fool of himself, or to observe a man in the so-called state of catalepsy, reposing like a marble statue between two chairs serving as a dubious support merely for his feet and head? Some demonstrators even place an additional weight on the body, sometimes quite considerable ("the more, the better," they would say), to bring out conspicuously the muscular rigidity of the body in a trance. Or witness the following demonstration, as described by Upton Sinclair:[1] "The hypnotist cries: 'You are drowning!'—and the youth begins splashing imaginary water, making frantic efforts to get to a non-existing shore. The audience roars with delight to see this youth in a position so far inferior to itself." Such spectacles commonly require a deep state, but they serve no scientific purpose.

I have found that scientific aims seldom call for a deep trance which, incidentally, can be attained only in 15% to 50% of subjects. In the past, the difficulty was generally regarded as a serious handicap to a full utilization of hypnotic "power." This is not necessarily the case. As a matter of fact, somnambulism is often undesirable, because the cooperation of the subject usually decreases with the deepening of the trance. This is particularly true of post-hypnotic suggestion. "The most perfect execution of post-hypnotic commands may be expected from such hypnotized persons as make the impression of being in full possession of their senses in spite of a high degree of suggestibility. Post-hypnotic indisposition is more pronounced in the case of the more complete degree of hypnosis as a rule. But an exception must be made for those hypnotized persons who seem to be acting, during hypnosis, in the world suggested to them, not much differently than in the waking state."[2] An explanation of this fact is easily found. It is obvious, of course, that unintelligent

[1] *What God Means to Me,* 35.
[2] Schilder and Kauders, *Hypnosis,* 5-6.

cooperation is of lesser value than cooperation based on a conscious and rational will. And deep hypnosis generally tends to make actions mechanical and irra-tional, and hence ineffectual in changed conditions. Furthermore, the subjects commonly resent any attempt on the part of the hypnotist to influence them in a way that does not meet their full approval. Consequently, the subject resents the suggestion and develops resist-ance and negativism.

Among the scientific hypnotists, the conviction was growing for some time that it is hardly an advantage for the psychological, educational, or even medical re-search and treatment to deal with an obedient but secretly disgruntled slave whose muscles are bound by the fetters of powerful inhibition or, to modify the analogy, to deal with a dummy unable to think, reason and criticize. Some authors, notably B. Sidis and, more recently, J. Goldwyn, went so far in the direction opposite to the popular tradition as to contend that the state of simple somnolence caused by the monotony of sensations and by the limitation of voluntary activities is sufficient for many therapeutic purposes. Somno-lence, it is true, may be all that is required in some cases, just as deep hypnosis may be needed in others. But in most instances, the advantages proffered by a closer contact with the autonomic nervous system are so great that a light trance is preferable whenever it can be pro-duced. For it combines an adequate control of the subject's bodily functions with his willingness and co-operation. I have come also to the conclusion that the prevailing tendency among hypnotists to stress muscular and sensory inhibitions—*not* to move this limb or that, *not* to see this object, *not* to hear that sound, *not* to feel

any pain—serves largely to conceal from scientific
attention the vast field of positive suggestion. It consists in stimulating, rather than in inhibiting, various
bodily and mental functions, as well as in removing
undesirable inhibitions. Positive suggestion cannot
always rely on mechanical obedience of the subject,
which is usually connected with somnambulism. It
often calls for an intense activity of the mind, in recalling forgotten experiences, in imagining new sensations,
in reasoning out problems, and in establishing fresh
forms of emotional conditioning. These purposes are
promoted by the clearness of the subject's mind. He
manifests a better response in a light trance.

So I proceeded to develop a state in which the subject's mind is instructed to remember, to think, to
criticize, in short, to be free and active; while the body
persists in the inhibited state, with an open channel connecting consciousness and the autonomic nervous
system. The procedure aimed simply to utilize every
advantage of the trance and to remove its common dis-
advantages.

The resulting form of light hypnosis I called
oneirosis, to indicate its kinship to somnolence and
slumber ("oneiros" means dream in Greek), rather
than to sleep ("hypnos," sleep) that often is an enduring dark emptiness, as far as memory and experience are
concerned.

As soon as the subject is informed, in the pre-
hypnotic stage, that he is going to be aware of everything that happens to him in the trance, that he will
subsequently recall distinctly his experiences in the state,
and that the state will end immediately upon command,
he is sincerely ready for cooperation. And such co-

operation is the best thing a practician should desire or hope to attain, provided he is willing at all times to be careful as to what he says, how he puts the words, what instructions he gives. For a critical subject will not readily obey nonsensical directions. Stupid tricks and ridiculous performances are not compatible with oneirosis, perhaps for the good of all concerned.

After the source of natural anxiety and distrust has thus been removed, and after every precaution to save the subject any unnecessary physical uneasiness has been taken, the subject is hypnotized in an ordinary fashion. Few people are ever annoyed by the state of hypnosis in general, but in reports on oneirosis the expressions of surprise and pleasure are particularly common. "It was a very enjoyable and agreeable state," writes one. "I felt like remaining that way for a long time," confesses another. "I did not want to come out of the state," asserts the third. "There seemed to be one thing that held my attention; it was the warm, joyous blood in my veins," states the fourth.

Let me cite a more detailed passage from one of my subject's reports: "There is no other state comparable to it. It is somewhat between a waking and a sleeping state—a drowsy, comfortable inertia envelops one. Regardless of the position taken, whether sitting, slouching, or reclining, during the state I feel utterly at ease. I have never had the desire to awaken nor to fall asleep—merely to continue in that state. There is no consciousness of the body, of the chair, of the room, of anything, except the voice, speaking, speaking, speaking. Under this state I am conscious of nothing, yet acutely aware of everything. The tick of the clock, the dropping of a pin, the window shade moving, the opening of the door, the mere change in pitch in Dr. Winn's voice—no change in the environment escapes me."

The subjects' reports themselves are an interesting novelty, rich in valuable introspective information, demonstrating that the subject in the state of oneirosis is distinctly critical and discriminative. After having been in the state but once, no one will maintain that hypnosis is necessarily oppression and enslavement.

For comparison, take the following description of oneirosis, dealing with a group experiment in education, by an objective outside observer, a newspaper reporter:[3] "A new approach to the problem of student attentiveness was demonstrated at City College last night by Dr. Ralph B. Winn, instructor in the Department of Philosophy and Psychology, who has developed a 'type of hypnosis in which the subject retains the free activity of the mind'.

"Dr. W., who calls the state produced oneirosis— the prefix meaning 'dream'—has been experimenting with a single volunteer student for several months, he made known. Last Wednesday, with a group of ten young men and women, who had received their parents' permission to participate, he began more formal tests, and last night, after some persuasion, allowed a few outsiders to watch and hear the new form of teaching.

"It was made plain that the 'course' is not a part of the college curriculum and that students get no credit for taking part. But Dr. W. said his results already had convinced him that not only were his subjects far more attentive than the average lecture-room student, but that their reactions, written down after they

---

[3] The *New York Times,* for February 22, 1934.

emerged from the oneirotic state showed better than usual retentiveness.

"The large, many-rowed lecture hall on the third floor of the main building on St. Nicholas terrace was devoted to the test after Dr. W. had delivered his usual two-hour lecture in an evening session class in abnormal psychology. When the regular students had left, A. S. and C. H., the psychologist's assistants for the experiment, brought in the apparatus.

"This was merely a series of light silvery balls, about the size of large marbles, each suspended on a ten-inch string from a thin metal rod. The rods were attached to the posts at the back of the seats, so that the spheres were suspended a short distance above the students' brows.

"Only seven of the ten volunteers were able to be present—four girls and three boys.

"Dr. W. at 9:51 began in a slow, slightly hushed voice: 'Take a comfortable position—and concentrate —your eyes on the gray ball above you. I want you to relax completely—and soon you'll fall into a state of oneirosis. I want you to relax completely—your hearts to beat evenly—to fall into a deeper state than you have ever fallen before—I want you to relax completely'.

"His words were evenly spaced, with a surprisingly soothing tone. At seven minutes to 10, the four students in the first row had closed their eyes and were breathing evenly and two of the three in the second row had done the same. Only M. S., a brunette, who later said she had been in a cramped position, still had her eyes open.

"But she too was 'asleep' in another minute and a

half and Dr. W. began his lecture, which concerned
eclipses, comets and meteors. At three minutes to ten,
S. H., in the first row, swallowed. At 10 sharp, S. N.,
at her side, opened his eyes and nodded once—but soon
closed them again. All of the others continued breathing regularly, a few with lips half parted.

"It was 10:09 when Dr. W. said, increasing the
volume in his tone: 'Let this be enough for tonight—
let the image dwell in your mind—but now I want you
to feel well—to feel completely well. Open your eyes.
Open your eyes. Open your eyes'.

"A few minutes later, the group was writing its
reactions—and then, answering questions.

"With only one exception, the students had recalled
vividly the details of the lecture. To Miss H., the
comet had been a 'strand of hair, with a bushy tail,
colored like electric light'. Only F. P., who admitted
he was somewhat of an experimenter himself, had seen
'no images at all'. At times, he said, he had heard no
voice, although he was certain he could have opened his
eyes if he desired."

As hypnosis is a state of high suggestibility, in which
the autonomic nervous system inhibits or stimulates
various mental and bodily activities or even capabilities;
and as it depends largely on the practician what changes
to produce in his subject and how to direct them—
oneirosis is not so much a new form of hypnosis as the
road toward modifying the hypnotic state so as to enable the scientist to do his psychological, educational, or
medical work, as the case may be, with the maximum
efficiency and success. The research along these lines
has only begun. Much, so unbelievably much, remains
to be done.

CHAPTER IX

THREE FIELDS OF PRACTICE

Among the practical fields in which suggestion and hypnosis can be successfully applied are medicine, psychology and education. In the first of these fields a considerable amount of experimental work has already been done, particularly by physicians and neurologists of France, England and Germany. Some interesting studies were recently undertaken in this country, of which the most outstanding are those of C. L. Hull and his associates, but here as elsewhere the research is being conducted largely at random and by guesswork, without sufficient directives of a comprehensive theory and without adequate controls of experimental technique. In psychology and education, on the other hand, even these signs of interest are lacking. This is really surprising, the more so that it is generally known that suggestion is highly successful in influencing human minds. Any experienced journalist, teacher, minister, statesman, or salesman can testify that, in favorable conditions, it is not very difficult to arouse human curiosity, to make people emotional, or to stimulate them to action. Many of us recall the propaganda of the Great War days, when men, women and children were aroused to an enthusiasm and hatred which they themselves would not comprehend today, when they listened to atrocity stories that would meet only with ridicule under normal conditions. The power of indoctrination is even more noticeable in our own times, especially when we acquaint ourselves with what is happening in Italy and Germany. These are all well known facts. Yet theory lags behind practice, and little is known of the precise manner in which suggestion works. Much patient and difficult experimentation is required to find, under conditions of scientific control, the adequate techniques to be used in various situations in which people's minds can be influenced and directed. But once such research goes under way and becomes thorough and systematic, who can tell how far it will lead? Is it really incorrect to maintain that suggestion is one of the mighty tools of education, which can be used for good purposes and evil? Is it wrong to assert that no leadership is effective on a large scale, unless it resorts to suggestion? As far as hypnosis is concerned, it may be superfluous in ordinary situations, but it is hard to overestimate its value in exceptional and pathological cases.

A. Medicine

The scientific significance of hypnotic suggestion was first demonstrated in surgery. One hundred years ago, as is well known, operations were extremely unsafe and brutal. As antisepsis was totally unheard of, infection, gangrene and death were their common results. People risked undergoing an operation only when they were virtually convinced that the only alternative was death. And indeed, mortality among surgical cases was so great that it is difficult to say whether more patients survived than died. To make things worse, all surgery was excruciatingly painful. Imagine yourself on the operating table, fully conscious and sensitive, while a surgeon removes your appendix, and several attendants hold your arms and legs!

Though anaesthetics (ether and nitrous oxide) were known from the beginning of the nineteenth century, they were not applied to surgical practice until much later. The first operation under ether was performed in 1842, but anaesthesia was not generally used until about 1850. As far as local anaesthesia is concerned, it (cocaine) was not discovered until 1884 by C. Koller. It was approximately at this time that Esdaile, a British surgeon in India, decided to try hypnosis. In the brief period of 1847–1851, he performed, on the natives, altogether several hundred operations, both minor and major. During the first year, he was not completely successful, and some of his patients suddenly awoke in the midst of an operation. But in the subsequent years he improved his technique, gained in confidence, and operated without any disturbance on the part of his patients.

It may be interesting to quote the description of one such operation performed by Esdaile's colleague, Dr. Webb, who spoke before the Medical College of Calcutta in these words: "I cannot recall without astonishment the extirpation of a cancerous eye, while the man looked at me unflinchingly with the other one. In another case, the patient looked dreamily on with half-closed eyes the whole time of the operation, even while I examined the nature of the malignant tumor I had removed, and then, having satisfied myself, concluded the operation."[1]

---

[1] As given by Bramwell in his *Hypnotism,* 19.

Surgery under hypnosis, doubtless, would have been practised more widely with time, had not the use of chemical anaesthesia spread during the subsequent years. It must be acknowledged that ether, chloroform and nitrous oxide have a considerable advantage over hypnosis. Unless the physician is a master of suggestion to start with, deep hypnosis is an exceedingly difficult tool: it may require years of training and experience, and even then one cannot be sure that every case will be one hundred percent successful. Ordinary anaesthetics, on the other hand, can be employed with great facility and certainty. Such was the situation which, unfortunately, made hypnosis impracticable, in its first bid for scientific recognition.

Hypnotic suggestion penetrated considerably slower the field of therapeutic medicine. Yet here its influence was more lasting, it seems. In the course of the last thirty or forty years, ample evidence has been accumulated to show that hypnosis can be successfully used in the treatment of many diseases, especially when they are rooted in neurotic disorders and complexes. The older evidence was carefully collected and discussed in detail in two books of the same title, *Hypnotism,* by A. Moll and J. M. Bramwell, but much additional material can be found in various scientific journals of recent date. Finally, the latest scientific findings were compiled and briefly discussed by H. F. Dunbar, in her *Emotions and Bodily Changes*.

Just to convey a general idea as to the progress of hypnotic therapy, I wish to give at this point a representative list of ailments that have been and can be relieved or cured by suggestion, whenever diagnosis indicates a functional cause:

Hysteria, in all forms
Morbid fears, obsessions and compulsions
Nervous tremors, tics and chorea
Neurasthenia
Insomnia
Speech disorders, including stammering

Sexual impotence
Frigidity
Disturbance of menstruation
Sex perversions
Masturbation
Nocturnal incontinence

Stomach aches
Indigestion
Constipation
Loss of appetite
Headaches
Sea sickness

Asthma, of nervous origin
Functional heart disorders
Neuralgia
Sciatica
Physical allergy (supersensitiveness) and hay fever
Eczema, in several forms

Chronic alcoholism
Drug addiction, such as morphinism

etc., etc.

Scientific literature is full also of isolated instances of successful treatment of other diseases; but such cases require further observation and verification. Anyway, the above list is long enough to give us a general idea as to the possibilities of hypnotic research and practice. Not being a physician and having made, consequently, few medicàl observations of my own, I shall limit myself to a single illustration. Several years ago I was closely associated with a distinguished scholar, Professor F., who suffered from a grave case of asthma. The disease took finally an acute form that threatened to interrupt a fruitful career. For months he was forced to abstain from all work and tiresome exercise, and still physicians failed to help. Then one day, as I was informed, he came across a Christian Scientist. I presume Dr. F. had despaired of medical assistance and was ready to try something new. People do become prone to be converted in the days of a health crisis. What transpired between the two, I do not exactly know. What is important here is that a prestige-and-faith relationship was evidently established between them, and suggestion was sufficient to effect a cure where medicine had failed to help. I regret only that the means of effecting it was not scientific.

There are several specific lines along which medical research should be continued, as the data already available are extremely promising. J. F. Woods, for instance, recommended hypnosis for lowering temperature in rheumatic fever, pleurisy and pneumonia. It may be used also to prevent arterio-sclerosis, whenever its development is due in part to constipation or gastric disorders. O. G. Wetterstrand contended that no remedy exerts so soothing an influence on the dying person as hypnotic suggestion. A. Munthe had an extensive practice along these lines and was able to report[2] that "even more striking is the beneficial effect of this method in the most painful of all operations, as a rule still to be endured without anaesthesia—Death. What it was granted to me to do for many of our dying soldiers during the last war is enough to make me thank God for having had this powerful weapon in my hands. In the autumn of 1915 I spent two unforgettable days and nights among a couple of hundred dying soldiers, huddled together under their bloodstained great-coats on the floor of a village church in France. We had no morphia, no chloroform, no anaesthetics whatever to alleviate their tortures and shorten their agony. Many of them died before my eyes, insensible and unaware, often even a smile on their lips, with my hand on their forehead, my slowly repeated words of hope and comfort resounding in their ears, the terror of death gradually vanishing from their closing eyes."

No less interesting are the possibilities offered by hypnosis in childbirth. A number of medical authorities, among them von Oettiger, J. Raefler, Schultze, and Mohr, advocated suggestion to facilitate labor, especially when the mother is psychologically opposed to having a baby. In commenting upon this question, Mohr said in effect: "There are a number of well authenticated cases in which the term of labor was fixed in hypnosis and the term kept. This offers a therapeutic possibility which is not surprising if one recalls how often psychic excitement exerts an accelerating or inhibiting influence on the process of labor. The

---

[2] *The Story of San Michele,* 316-17.

extent to which the normal course of labor may be disturbed by psychic factors is seen perhaps most readily in cases where, because of complete distraction of attention, the automatic course of the process is not inhibited, i.e., in psychotic patients.   A woman whose earlier deliveries could be handled only instrumentally can give birth easily in abnormally short time to a child of the same weight, after she has become mentally ill (this is something to which Bleuler also has called attention.)"[3]

It is only fair to acknowledge, in this connection, that the above observations and experiments, conducted by individual physicians, cannot be regarded as the final word of investigation.   Opinions differ, in fact, on the subject.   Let me quote, for instance, from a recent statement issued by Dr. M. Fishbein, editor of the American Medical Association Journal: "Hypnotism has been used repeatedly for many years in an endeavor to alleviate the pains of childbirth but has not been found successful except in the case of hysterical individuals who have been repeatedly hypnotized and are therefore especially amenable to the power of suggestion."   This, too, represents but a partisan belief. We must await experiments on a larger scale, capable of providing decisive evidence as to whether hypnosis can, indeed, help to combine the painlessness of "twilight sleep" and the flexible obedience to the physician's orders.   In my mind there remains no doubt that it can. But we shall not have to wait long, perhaps, until this question is decided, one way or another.   A big experiment, I hear, is being conducted in Soviet Russia, and

---

[3] Quoted by H. F. Dunbar in *Emotions and Bodily Changes*, 344.

one of these days prospective mothers may get glad news.

Another interesting possibility lies in the field of abortion, where the intended results should be obtainable with greater ease and safety to the patient by means of hypnosis than with the help of drugs and surgery. Nor is this really surprising. As H. F. Dunbar reports, the connection between the mental state and the resulting abortion has been known for years. Kohts commented upon it, in referring to the great number of abortions and miscarriages during the bombardment of Strassburg in 1870. Baudelocque noticed the same phenomenon, when 92 cases of abortion came to him for treatment immediately after the explosion of a powder tower. Kalichmann, Schaeffer, Mayer, S. H. Prince, and others made similar observations. Obviously, the period of pregnancy is easily affected, from beginning to end, by emotion as well as by suggestion.

The records from which all the above data are taken are still further substantiated by indirect evidence. In this respect, clinical observations and theoretical considerations fully agree. We are justified, namely, in believing that any malady which is known to have been relieved, in some instances, by faith-healing or psychoanalysis, is likely to yield also to a proper hypnotic treatment. Unfortunately, we do not often know exactly what this treatment should be. Our information concerning the techniques required to assure success is still sadly lacking, and much research work is needed to find and determine them in detail.

In order to grasp clearly the possibilities as well as the limitations of hypnotic treatment, let us keep one fundamental rule in mind that might help us escape the temptations of superstition and mysticism. It may be put in the words of John Hunter, English physiologist, who said[4] that "as one state of the mind is capable of producing a disease, another state of the mind effects a cure." To put it more specifically, hypnosis as a curative agency should be applied only to those bodily disturbances and mental ailments which are directly or closely connected and regulated by the autonomic nervous system. Suggestion does not perform miracles, let it be understood once for all. It is completely helpless in maladies rooted in anatomical defects or in physiological troubles basically independent of the involuntary system. It is, indeed, foolish to hope that hypnosis will cure diphtheria, syphilis, or appendicitis. Fully recognizing these obvious limitations, we should not at the same time forget that there exist cases, quite numerous in fact, in which the symptom has merely the appearance of an anatomical defect, as in hysterical blindness, deafness or paralysis. The physician should remain strictly scientific in his diagnosis and know how to differentiate between these psychic ailments and similar organic maladies that require ordinary surgery or are totally incurable.

It seems to be a simple expectation that medical men abstain from non-scientific attitudes. Yet we occasionally meet physicians and scholars, some of them distinguished, even renowned, who still maintain a mystic attitude of mind toward their science. I was surprised and disappointed to find Alexis Carrel, a Nobel prize winner, among their number. Witness a statement from his *Man the Unknown*:[5] "Our present conception

---

[4] As quoted by Coué in his *Conscious Autosuggestion,* 29.
[5] Pp. 149-150.

of the influence of prayer upon pathological lesions is based upon the observation of patients who have been cured almost instantaneously of various affections, such as peritoneal tuberculosis, cold abscesses, osteitis, suppurating wounds, lupus, cancer, etc. The process of healing changes little from one individual to another. Often, an acute pain. Then a sudden sensation of being cured. In a few seconds, a few minutes, at the most a few hours, wounds are cicatrized, pathological symptoms disappear, appetite returns. Sometimes functional disorders vanish before the anatomical lesions are repaired. The skeletal deformations of Pott's disease, the cancerous glands, may still persist two or three days after the healing of the main lesions. The miracle is chiefly characterized by an extreme acceleration of the processes of organic repair. There is no doubt that the rate of cicatrization of the anatomical defects is much greater than the normal one. The only condition indispensable to the occurrence of the phenomenon is prayer. But there is no need for the patient himself to pray, or even to have any religious faith. It is sufficient that some one around him be in a state of prayer. Such facts are of profound significance. They show the reality of certain relations, of still unknown nature, between psychological and organic processes. They prove the objective importance of the spiritual authorities, which hygienists, physicians, educators, and sociologists have almost always neglected to study."

With all the respect due to Dr. Carrel, I feel forced emphatically to maintain that he does not speak of facts, not in the scientific sense of the word at least, when he discusses miracles. I have no objection to his attitude of faith. Any scientist has the right to believe the way he chooses. But he could keep faith and science separate and acknowledge that he is unable to bridge the gap between them. Dr. Carrel did not have to subscribe to the "absent treatments" doctrine of Christian Scientists. Courageously yet unwisely, he produced an unacceptable mixture of scientific and mystic language. Either can be used with logic and success, but the mixture and combination of both do not make sense.

Personally, I believe that there is an excellent scientific explanation of mystic psychology and of the remarkable effects it produces. I am not dogmatic enough to deny that faith can produce wonders. But there are special physiological reasons for that. There is no mystery in the inhibitory or stimulatory effects of the activity of the autonomic nervous system, when aroused by an intense religious experience. But it is obvious that, unless the man afflicted with a serious disease be himself affected by suggestion, the prayer of another person cannot bring about healing effects. Surely the autonomic nervous system of one man does not control that of another. To say so, or to imply so, is to show regrettable ignorance, from the scientific point of view, as to where science begins and where it ends.

B. Psychology

Hypnosis has just as great a variety of uses in psychology as it has in medicine. The practical success of suggestion—whether it be political propaganda, salesmanship, or educational indoctrination—testifies to this effect. A great majority of subjects appearing before the psychologist for treatment by suggestion suffer from some neurosis or, at least, from some complex. These mental ailments, incidentally, have spread enormously in the years of depression, thereby demonstrating their close connection with conditions of life. Now, it is extremely important for the hypnotist to determine the cause of his subject's troubles, as its removal might be sufficient to produce a complete cure. Suggestion cannot be effectively used without discrimination, as a panacea. In many instances, the source of a nervous malady lies in some physical ailment that should be taken care of before hypnosis is resorted to. In these cases it is advisable to secure the assistance of a competent physician or, as the case may be, of a surgeon. If the subject, for instance, is afflicted with a bodily deformity creating a serious handicap to his happiness or career, a plastic surgeon is sometimes able to correct the physical fault and, as a result, to remove a mental handicap to the subject's normal social relations.

In other instances, the subject is a victim of an unfavorable early environment, unfortunate experiences, marital difficulties, sex frustration. Here a qualified and experienced psychologist might be consulted. Or the subject should be given an opportunity to tell his life story at length and thus to find relief in conversational catharsis. If the case is rooted in some incorrigible physical defect bearing heavily upon the patient's mind—such as exceptionally bad looks, short stature, unusual fatness unyielding to sound diet—the possibilities for re-directing his interests should be investigated in order to provide him with a freer and more successful outlet for whatever abilities he may possess.

Music, scientific research, nursing, and political work can be recommended as some of the best fields for sublimation of one's physical and mental energies. A hypnotic treatment may or may not be required to assure good results of catharsis and sublimation.

Objectionable physical habits, such as nail-biting or lip-twitching, ordinarily call for strong suggestion. But in these cases, too, the hypnotist should keep in mind the possibility that the habit is merely a manifestation of nervousness and should not be treated apart from the underlying causes. If these be not removed, the habit, though apparently cured, is likely to come back before long, or to take an entirely different form. Hysterics, particularly, show this tendency to the return of symptoms of their disease. Whenever nervousness is not marked, however, one sitting or more, depending on the kind and gravity of the case, will often suffice to obliterate the fault completely. Unfortunately, in the absence of available precise techniques for every kind of trouble, the hypnotist is commonly forced to experiment and to devise his methods of treatment almost at a minute's notice. Naturally, these methods are not always as effective as they could be, had an extensive scientific experimentation preceded. Nevertheless, even at the present stage in the development of scientific hypnotism, certain general rules as well as certain specific methods can be laid down.

The first principle in treating objectionable habits is to condition the subject to some powerful emotion. Disgust and fear seem to be most effective, in this respect. But other emotions can be employed as well, either pleasant or unpleasant, as the case requires. Pre-hypnotic suggestions are useful, but the practician should concentrate more extensively on suggestions during the trance. Not to repeat the common but faulty practice of amateurs, the hypnotist should avail himself of, rather than violate, the rules of everyday psychological approach. Thus, it is not enough to reiterate, however vehemently, statements like "You are disgusted with your habit. You hate it. You will do your best to overcome it." Rather, one should utilize Pavlov's discovery, extensively applied to human beings by K. Dunlap, that a deliberate and repeated stimulation tends to extinguish a conditioned reflex. If the subject has, for instance, the habit of biting his nails, he is urged, while in the trance, to bite his nails consciously and repeatedly. At the same time, this procedure is associated with the feeling of disgust. Light hypnosis (oneirosis) is, of course, preferable to achieve the intended results.

The typical progress of improvement in a case of nail-biting is described in the following report written by a subject of mine, S. K., who received but one treatment:

"*Wednesday, November 8, 1933.*

"The first few hours after the experiment were not out of the ordinary. I did not try to bite my nails, but I believe this was more from will power than anything else, because my mind was constantly on my nails.

"*Thursday, November 9, 1933.*

"The experiment seems to be working with quite a good deal of efficiency. I filed my nails, and rounded them off. My mind was not on my nails, and only once, when I saw an uneven curve, did I feel like biting it to round it off. However, I used the file.

"*Friday, November 10, 1933.*

"Nothing unusual. I do not recall thinking of nails during the day, nor have I any recollection of trying to bite them.

"*Saturday, November 11, 1933.*

"I was asked how my nails were since the experiment. I looked at them, and found that they looked better than at any time for the past four or five years. Still have no desire to bite them, even to round them off. I just recalled that I used to bite them when I was excited over something, and that since Wednesday I have been excited over several things, and did not try to bite the nails.

"*Sunday, November 12, 1933.*

"I have been typing all afternoon, so I did not have the chance to bite them except during a period when I stopped to listen to the New York Philharmonic Symphony play Tchaikowsky's 'Pathétique', and then I was too busy enjoying the music to think of biting the nails.

"*Monday, November 13, 1933.*

"I have just looked at my nails, and have found one that is split near the edge. I started to bite it off, and then remembered that I wasn't supposed to. As soon as I finish writing this, I am going to use my file to even that off.

"*Tuesday, November 14, 1933.*

"I've been too busy to think of the experiment or to bite my nails. Only once, I caught myself trying to bite them, but I attribute this to a nervous reaction after being very busy for several hours without a let-up. Otherwise, there was nothing unusual.

"Wednesday, November 15, 1933.

"I've been wearing gloves, as I have been out a good part of the day, but I have felt no inclination to bite my nails.

"General Comment.

"As I have told you, before this experiment, every time I looked at my nails, I was tempted to bite them, but now I no longer have this inclination."

Personality faults present an even more fertile ground for suggestion and hypnosis. They are extremely wide spread and tenacious, and countless people can be benefitted by having them removed, as they commonly determine one's course of life and often decide whether it will be successful or not. Particularly useful it is to check their formation at an early age. Children, we may recall, can be hypnotized as easily as, if not easier than, adults.

Most personality faults are grounded in frustrations due to conditions of existence. The success of treatment is not assured, of course, so long as the conditions responsible for the trouble are not removed. It is foolish, therefore, to make suggestions which are bound to be defeated by the continuation of harmful influences which had produced the fault in the first place and which cannot be removed or modified by the subject himself. Any attempt to do so is not unlike a physician's advice to his poor anaemic patient burdened with family responsibilities to "take it easy" and to go away to Florida or California for a winter's rest. Nevertheless, in many instances, a hypnotic treatment, used intelligently and discriminately, can relieve the subject from that lack of confidence in his behavior which has weakened his social relations and aggravated his case

still further.   Much better results should be expected,
of course, whenever unfavorable conditions responsible
for the subject's troubles are, or can be made, a thing of
the past.   Among the faults usually yielding to suggestion or hypnosis, but requiring repeated sittings as a
rule, are the following:

Stage-fright and uneasiness in addressing the public
Fear of examinations
Excessive blushing
Shyness in specific circumstances
Various forms of inferiority

Poor handwriting
Incorrect posture in sitting or walking
Faults of pronunciation
Nervous stuttering

etc., etc.

Auto-suggestion is of considerable assistance in cor-
recting personality faults.   Though E. Coué, whose
popular acclaim fifteen or twenty years ago still lingers
in many minds, had little to contribute to our understanding of the nature of suggestion, practically he was
on the right track in urging his followers to cultivate
self-confidence as the key to a successful life. He used to
say:[6]

"Whoever starts off in life with the idea: 'I shall
succeed', does succeed because he does what is necessary
to bring about this result. If only one opportunity pre-

---

[6] "Thoughts and Precepts," *Self-Mastery through Conscious Auto-suggestion,* 1922. p. 38.

sents itself to him, and if this opportunity has, as it were, only one hair on its head, he seizes it by that one hair. Further, he often brings about unconsciously or not, propitious circumstances.

"He who on the contrary always doubts himself never succeeds in doing anything. He might find himself in the midst of an army of opportunities, with heads of hair like Absalom, and yet he would not see them and could not seize a single one, even if he had only to stretch out his hand in order to do so. And if he brings about circumstances, they are generally unfavorable ones. Do not then blame fate, you have only yourself to blame."

Despite the general correctness of this observation, E. Coué partly misunderstood and partly overestimated the power of independent auto-suggestion. In the popular mind, his name is associated with the famous formula, "Every day in every way I am getting better and better," supposedly a panacea, an efficient remedy against practically any disease. But the subsequent passing of the vogue, followed by the downfall of Coué's School, is a sufficient proof of the inadequacy of the precept. His temporary success was due, it seems, to the startling and powerful impression his lectures and books had made on the public, an impression which gradually faded, leaving the curative formula enfeebled, though still occasionally helpful. Obviously, it was founded on human faith and an individual's prestige. It remains true that only a small minority of men have a sufficient fountain of steady belief within themselves to transform undecisiveness into confidence, emotionality into calmness, timidity into courage. Even this minority have not enough faith to work upon themselves without guidance by some trusted authority. Auto-suggestion, far too commonly, calls for an outside inspiration or support.

As E. Jones has said,[7] "it is extraordinarily difficult to draw any sharp line between hetero- and auto-suggestion. The relationship is so very intimate as to make it probable that the agents operating in the two cases are merely variants and not distinct forces." There is, however, a quite definite reason for this intimacy. It is not necessary to believe that the source of auto-suggestion lies within the subject, whereas the source of hetero-suggestion resides solely in the practician. Even when one's mind appears to act spontaneously, external influences may play an important role; and when it seems to follow only the orders of another person, one's individual tendencies may be really responsible for the behavior. The entire controversy as to whether all auto-suggestion is actually hetero-suggestion, or vice versa, is futile, as both involve almost identical forces, though aroused in two different fashions.

As we have already seen, the physiological mechanism of suggestion (including that under hypnosis) is identical with the autonomic nervous system, together with its various connections. Scholars like S. Ferenczi are right, therefore, in believing that the energy operative in suggestion comes not from the practician but from the subject himself. In hypnotic treatment, this mechanism is not brought into action spontaneously, of course, but is stimulated through the channels of the central nervous system, as expressed in listening, watching, reading, etc. The starting point of suggestion is

---

[7] "The Nature of Auto-Suggestion," *The British Journal of Medical Psychology*, 1923. p. 205.

to be looked for, ordinarily, in sensory experience, but the resulting complexity of involuntary activities may be determined by subsequent deliberation and emotional reaction of the subject himself (auto-suggestion) or be precipitated by ideas and emotions conveyed from outside sources (hetero-suggestion). In the latter case, the stimulation may come through deliberate efforts of a single individual or as the reflection of a group or crowd attitude. Panic in a burning theater is a fitting example of mass suggestion. McDougall offers us an illuminating comment:[8] "If I meet an angry bear in the woods and take to my heels in fear, it would be true to say that the energy which sustains my efforts comes from within my organism, and is not in any sense supplied by the bear; the bear merely releases this energy within me. But it would not be true or useful to say that my fear was self-inspired and that the bear had nothing to do with the case or played but a secondary role in the drama."

Once we comprehend this nature of the mechanism of suggestion, it is not difficult to infer that what is known as auto-suggestion can be used apart from somebody inspiring the subject only in exceptional cases. Ordinarily, it should not be practised without the assistance of a qualified practician. A specialist is required not only to supervise, but also to inspire the subject. However, once the prestige-and-faith relationship is established and sufficiently strengthened, a mere recollection of the hypnotist's recommendations may be enough to stimulate the subject's autonomic system to action, again and again. Here lies the practical significance of

---

[8] *Outline of Abnormal Psychology*, 123.

the method of auto-suggestion in its post-hypnotic application.

Every physician knows, or should know, from experience that the prestige he commands serves not only as a means of building up his practice, but also as a valuable tool for overcoming his patients' ailments. Ridiculous as the assumption may seem at a first glance, the way he speaks, his manners, his clothes, even his automobile are often influential in restoring people to health. A patient's faith in his doctor is frequently no less useful than the drug he prescribes. Most physicians do not quite comprehend the theoretical foundations of human prestige. Yet, in the last analysis, what is prestige but popular faith and respect? Is it not a form of auto-suggestion on a large scale, with the autonomic nervous system controlling the bodily aspect of the attitude? The same truth, though in a somewhat different manner, applies to the lawyer's practice and to the teacher's instruction. All of them cannot help but deal in suggestion and, for their own sake, should prepare minds for its reception. Let then the reasons for their influence upon people's minds be not merely a lesson of personal experience, but also a scientific fact of human psychology, that can be utilized in a thousand ways to improve the effectiveness of professional work.

The only type of auto-suggestion based on no distinct prestige-and-faith relationship, yet truly effective, is *rationalization*. It is essentially wish-thinking and consists in modifying and distorting one's opinions, judgments, and perceptions to conform them to one's preestablished likes and dislikes or to justify one's previously expressed statements. When a mother, listening to quarreling children, takes the side of her own boy, she is not deliberately unjust. Her partiality is sincere, but it is a result of rationalization nevertheless. Wish-thinking, by virtue of which one is usually right while the opponent is usually wrong, is an everyday phenomenon, and no one is entirely free from it. It molds one's reaction to events, it permeates one's political activities, it determines one's choice of books and entertainment, it decides the questions of love and hatred. Auto-suggestion, in the form of rationalization, is indeed a universal trait, and no social psychologist dares to disregard it. But, of course, for better or for worse, rationalization is self-deception.

A few words should be said, in the conclusion of this section, about the use of hypnosis as an aid to theoretical psychology. It can be employed with advantage in studying memory, perception, imagination, and emotion, both normal and abnormal, as we have already had an opportunity to see. These and other fields of human behavior provide an inexhaustible source of themes for specific studies and experiments. Very little research has been attempted so far along these lines. But we observe, among scientists, a growing interest in hypnosis, and occasionally we come across an article or a note dealing with it. For instance, an interesting study has been done in dreams, conducted by D. B. Klein. Some of his conclusions deserve to be quoted in full:[9]

"Hypnotic dreams can be elicited by stimuli embracing a wide range of sense modalities.

"Verbal stimuli serve as effective instigation of hypnotic dreams. . .

"The reality of dreamless sleep being an amnesic

---

[9] "The Experimental Production of Dreams during Hypnosis," University of Texas Bulletin No. 3009, 1930.

phenomenon, at least for some persons, was experimentally demonstrated. . .

"Dreaming during hypnosis . . . is the same in kind and mechanism as ordinary night dreaming. . . .

"Direct examination of the hypnotic dreams fail to reveal any additional characteristic that would serve to differentiate them from non-hypnotic dreams."

There is no reason why hypnosis should not be applied in such a way to countless other problems, whenever its possible usefulness is indicated. Hypnotism, old as it is in irregular practice, is a newcomer to science and a very deserving and promising one. Superstition, either in favor of it or in opposition to it, is a vicious obstacle to the advance of knowledge.

C. Education

The field of education is totally new to the hypnotist. The little work which I have done in it, however, has made me appreciate its potential significance. Though it is too early as yet to draw any specific conclusions from my experimental research begun several years ago, nevertheless certain general and fairly obvious considerations left no doubt in my mind that suggestion, ordinary and hypnotic, is of inestimable value for the school.

The traditional method of teaching consisted in indoctrinating the young people with a set of customary but "respectable"—and hence obsolescent—ideas, with little if any appreciation of the student's character, interests, and personal environment. As long as the pupils were, for the most part, members of the privileged class, they could be satisfied with such an academic polish; in fact, it differentiated them from *hoi poloi*. But as the spirit of democracy penetrated the schools and opened the academic gates to the masses, both the curriculum and pedagogic methods had to be modified to meet the new demands and conditions. The change was inevitable. Yet institutions, as so often happens in the face of a clear trend, manifested a social lag. And the school system refused to yield. Educators themselves were reluctant to adjust their practices to the march of time. As to the community leaders, they were as a rule inimical to serious alterations in the system. Under the pressure of circumstances, however, some changes were forced upon the school, yet even so they were commonly belated and inadequate. To some extent, the conditions still prevail. Today, many of us realize that Latin should have been dropped as a compulsory course at least one hundred years before the concession was actually made; that mathematics should be taught as a practical subject for realistic purposes; that history should have been re-written to throw light on contemporary events; that athletics should have been adapted to promote students' health and sportsmanship, not to raise funds for the alma mater; that learning for social usefulness should have supplanted study for personal distinction. Above all, the educator should comprehend that the students' interest is the vehicle of real knowledge and the principal criterion of his own success or failure in the capacity of teacher and representative of the system.

Drama and suggestion are the two vitalizing powers underlying all effective learning. To make education fruitful, the students must be made aware of the significance of their work. Otherwise they will direct their attention elsewhere and study to get grades, credits, degrees, or pursue other objectives, relevant or irrelevant to education, that they will discover in their academic work. Drama and suggestion, I repeat, are the two vitalizing powers underlying all effective learning. There can be no drama about subjects dead to the student, and suggestion is bound to be sterile unless problems presented to the class are exciting. The process of learning is fruitful only in so far as it is akin to life itself and draws constantly from life's changing issues and stresses. And who but the teacher is qualified to reveal and explain to the student the meaning of his environment and his relationship between the individual and society?

That human personalities are molded by suggestion, will be generally admitted. Take, for instance, the art of advertising. A business man, in offering his products on the market, will not describe their qualities, good and bad, in an objective manner; rather, he will dwell on the attractive, exclusive, important features and thus try to arouse human attention and desire. A sign or a slogan does not impose, it suggests. And people yield to it, if it is built and presented according to the rules of popular psychology. These facts are appreciated in the business world to such an extent that, despite the colossal expense of education by advertising, no firm or industry can afford to neglect it.

Business men have grasped this lesson in educating the public by suggestion. They know full well that public taste is directed by being whetted. But our high schools and colleges still continue to resort to the old-fashioned methods of dry assignment and recitation, with almost a complete disregard of psychology and common sense. As a result, class work is notoriously boring and ineffective, education being achieved, as it were, despite the educators' efforts, in extra-curricular activities rather than in the class-room. Some people would not believe the tragedy of this situation, but let them ask schoolboys and schoolgirls. If these are intelligent, observant and frank, the truth will be told.

The school is thus lagging behind business in appreciating the value of suggestion in learning. This fault should be corrected. There are two types of suggestion that can be used with advantage in educational work. A great majority of students can be aroused to hard study by up-to-date information about natural and social sciences, in a dramatic form; by appealing to their personal interests; by a wealth of concrete examples; by an intelligent approach to their emotions and imagination; and in a hundred other ways. The life-like suggestiveness of facts drawn directly from experience and reality and cleverly presented, is all they really require. In such cases, hypnosis can not, and ought not to, be used as a substitute for regular educational practices.

Then again there are individuals who, for various reasons, fail to respond to simple suggestion by words and example. They may be victims of unfortunate experiences that had conditioned them wrongly to school work; they may be suffering from some form of neurosis; they may be affected by some bodily or mental idiosyncrasy, putting them into a class by themselves. In quite a few of these cases, hypnosis can be of valuable service, either in freeing the individual from his psychological difficulties or in stimulating his interests, which refuse to be aroused in normal ways. Imagination, particularly, is a capacity which admits of great intensification through hypnotic (oneirotic) suggestion and can be utilized in many different ways to facilitate pedagogic purposes.

Not all fields of learning are equally adapted to hypnotic suggestion. There is hardly any great future for it in ordinary sciences, such as mathematics, history, economics, or physics.[10] Much more promising, in this respect, are arts and skills in which emotion, particularly fear, are involved. Take, for instance, stage-fright or self-consciousness in public appearances. Everybody knows its psychological effects. One's memory is ready, one is willing and anxious to act according to one's best ability; but something happens the moment one appears on the stage: movements become clumsy, voice trembling, and memory refuses to perform its normal service. Clearly, it is a case of inhibition, and often a rather ridiculous sight. Stage-fright is due, of course, to lack of confidence and is anything but useful to the performer. It deprives the speaker of that "at-home" attitude on the platform which is essential to the stage. It makes the actor self-conscious and, therefore, unnatural in his behavior precisely at the time when mental and bodily ease are a condition of his success. Both the cause and the cure of these wide-spread difficulties are psychological. Practice may help. But there is no better remedy for them than hypnotic treatment.

The phenomenon of stage-fright affects not only actors; it is familiar in many walks of life. I recall my first experience in public lecturing. It was during my first or second year of graduate work at the University

---

[10] Even here hypnosis is not without value, as demonstrated by D. M. Allan's experiments on 60 college students.

of Southern California. A large club of society women asked my department to send them a speaker. For some reason I was chosen. There was enough time for preparing the lecture, and I spent a great many hours in selecting and arranging material for it. Finally, the day has arrived, and I was ready and on time. The chairman asked me to say a few words about my experiences abroad, and then added a few flattering words of introduction. But once I faced the audience, I forgot all about the chairman's suggestion and went immediately on with my lecture, just as it had been prepared. I did not see anything, I did not hear anything, I was just rattling on with my speech—until the lecture was over. The ladies were quite encouraging in their applause. But I must have been, I know, a rather amusing sight. Was my experience exceptional? Certainly not. Stage-fright is a psychological attitude affecting, and embarrassing to, many people. And consequently, hypnosis can be of help to:

> Actors
> Singers
> Musicians
> Radio speakers
> Orators
> Lecturers
> Lawyers
> Students
>
> etc., etc.

There are also activities requiring a certain amount of self-confidence to start with, and fear or uncertainty may present a serious handicap. Everybody finds among his friends a number of people unable to swim, for instance. Were swimming a skill acquired only after considerable training, this should be expected. But the facts are quite different. Most animals who fall into the water usually have no great difficulty in scrambling out and learning how to swim as a result. Boys and girls are hardly different in this respect. The art of swimming comes to them naturally, in due course of time, unless the fear of water is suggested to them. But some adults simply can't acquire the skill, no matter what they do. A deliberate effort to learn how to swim has, it seems, no advantage over an accidental fall into deep water. An acquaintance of mine once assured me that she can swim in four feet of water; but the moment she gets into a deeper place, she goes down like a stone. Ridiculous, is it not? Yet she cannot help it; like so many other people, she is wrongly conditioned to swimming. There is but one method of fighting against this fault, and it is to modify the psychological attitude and to inspire the subject with confidence, be it only for the few moments of retraining. Hypnosis can be of obvious assistance in such cases.

Swimming is but one of many skills depending on self-confidence in the first minutes, hours or days of practice. Hypnosis can be, no doubt, successfully employed in teaching how to master the following skills:

To swim
To skate
To ride a bicycle
To ride a horse
To drive a car
To dance

etc., etc.

I do not mean, of course, that hypnotic suggestion should be used in *all* instruction in the above activities. Quite the contrary, it should be resorted to only in *exceptional* cases, when a particular inability is clearly caused by a psychological attitude of fear or uncertainty and, consequently, by an inhibition. In fact, I do not recommend the application of hypnosis on a large scale. It should remain a powerful tool used with caution and discrimination.

Conclusions

Men lived by feeling and faith long before they began to reason. In those early days, there was no knowledge, in the modern sense of the word, no inquiries into the nature and causes of things. People simply had beliefs and asked no questions. When they believed strongly, they felt strongly; they felt with every muscle and every tissue within them. Faith may not move mountains literally, but since ancient days it has moved every important organ in the body. And suggestion is the vehicle of faith, passing it from man to man, arousing crowds, spreading from chiefs down to their followers, rising from people up to their chosen leaders. Rooted in primitive tendencies, suggestion reaches deeper than most of us know. It is a power hard to measure and hard to control.

It is precisely because the power of suggestion and faith are akin that the field of hypnotism was one of the last to be emancipated from mysticism, which is faith intellectualized. The phenomena of suggestion appeal to feeling and blind belief. Especially when strong faith resulted in strange cures, how could people, ignorant people, refrain from taking them for miracles and from acclaiming the persons capable of performing these wonders as possessed of divine powers? Who could conquer the emotions naturally going with faith and regard the facts of suggestion coldly and speculatively?

Before a field of knowledge can be turned systematically to human advantage, it must be comprehended, and the laws controlling it found. Thus, the forces of electricity could be canalized only when they became a subject of intense study and careful experimentation. Similarly, the powers of suggestion can be directed to serve mankind only when superstition is banned and forgotten. Science begins where mysticism ends.

The habits of exact observation and logical thinking are being slowly established among men, and field after field begins to be studied with a scientific attitude of mind. And research men gradually learn to trace phenomena of suggestion into the tissues of the organism. More and more, they comprehend the ways of the body and of the mind, in their mutual dependence.

As one of these research men, I am anxious to help in transforming the art of suggestion into a science and in providing a scientific foundation for the study of hypnosis. I do not believe that I have retained many prejudices of the past. And I am quite certain that no mysticism vitiates my thinking. So I wrote this book. As to positive results attained in the course of my studies, the following summary is offered for consideration:

1. Most people, in getting acquainted with hypnosis, usually take a prejudicial attitude to it: they are aroused either to idle curiosity and enthusiasm or to unjustified contempt and disregard of the phenomena.

2. The truth is, however, that hypnotic phenomena are as natural as those of physics, biology, or economics.

3. Hence, the proper scientific attitude is to seek the explanation and control of hypnosis.

4. Such study has two important aspects: the psychological aspect and the physiological one.

5. On the psychological side, hypnosis consists in arousing ideas, images and emotions by means of suggestion.

6. In fact, hypnosis invariably implies suggestion and its human source, a hypnotist.

7. For its effectiveness, suggestion depends on the intensity of a prestige-and-faith relationship established between the practician and his subject.

8. The use of suggestion is not new, of course, in influencing people's minds and in curing their maladies, particularly hysteria: it was commonly employed by faith-healers and their modern successors.

9. Hypnosis offers today a splendid opportunity to put suggestion under scientific control and to utilize its beneficent powers according to the best knowledge of our times.

10. On the physiological side, hypnosis involves functions of the autonomic nervous system, together with its various connections.

11. The autonomic nervous system controls and regulates the mechanical activities of the body, exemplified by digestion.

12. These activities are not open to any direct control of the conscious will.

13. But they are sometimes considerably modified by interference of emotions and suggestions, which constitute the two channels bridging the voluntary and the involuntary nervous systems.

14. Many bodily functions, ordinarily controlled by the autonomic nervous system, become stimulated or

inhibited under the influence of suggestion and, particularly, of hypnosis.

15.   The bodily mechanism underlying the disease of hysteria as well as some of the successful practices of faith-healers, Christian Scientists, and psycho-analysts is identical with that of all suggestion: it is rooted in the autonomic nervous system.

16.   Bringing the psychological and the physiological aspects together, we can define the hypnotic state as a prestige-and-faith relationship in which the practician uses his advantageous position to influence by suggestion the subject's autonomic nervous system, in order to effect desired bodily inhibitions and excitations and to condition his mind.

17.   All hypnotic practice is remarkably safe, at least in the hands of an experienced, intelligent and honest practician.

18.   The young science of hypnotism calls for numerous experiments, as specified techniques are sadly lacking to deal with the great variety of medical, psychological and educational cases.

19.   The scientific study of hypnotic phenomena is, indeed, in an early stage, but its future is bright and promising.

INDEX OF NAMES